Getting more sorted!

more

∧

your health

your education

your independence

your work

your home

Published by
British Association for Adoption & Fostering
(BAAF)
Saffron House
6-10 Kirby Street
London EC1N 8TS
www.baaf.org.uk

Charity registration 275689

British Library Cataloguing in Publication Data
A catalogue record for this book is available from the British Library

ISBN 1 905664 11 7

Written by Rebecca Davidson
Project management by Shaila Shah, Director of Publications, BAAF
Illustrations by Fran Orford
Designed by Andrew Haig & Associates
Printed in Great Britain by The Lavenham Press
Trade distribution by Turnaround Publisher Services, Unit 3, Olympia
Trading Estate, Coburg Road, London N22 6TZ

BAAF is the leading UK-wide membership organisation for all those
concerned with adoption, fostering and child care issues.

Acknowledgements

 The initial idea for this publication and the text were commissioned and sponsored by Woodside Fostercare, who are delighted with the subsequent development which has led to this guide.

The text for this guide was written by Rebecca Davidson with input from Henrietta Bond.

We would like to thank Marion Hundleby, JoAnne Salmon and her colleagues at Fostering People, Nottingham, and Samina Akhtar at A National Voice for reading and commenting on the text. Thanks also to Larry, Barry and Danny for offering useful suggestions on the illustrations.

Note about the author

Rebecca Davidson worked for several years as Support Services Co-ordinator for an independent foster care association, with responsibility for co-ordinating and overseeing therapy and education provision. She currently specialises in working with people with special educational needs, in particular those with autism and Asperger Syndrome.

Note about the illustrator

The cartoons in this book were drawn by Fran Orford. Fran's cartoons have been used in over 70 magazines and newspapers in both the UK and abroad, including *The Observer, Private Eye* and *The Telegraph*. Before becoming a cartoonist Fran set up and ran a Leaving Care Team for NCH in Halifax, West Yorkshire, and before that he worked with homeless and disadvantaged teenagers in London.

Contents

Introduction

Preparing to move on

Becoming an adult is one of the biggest steps we take in our lives. The time between being a young person and becoming an adult is often called "transition" which means a journey or a crossing from one place to another. This book will help you prepare for this journey so that you can arrive at the other side ready to live as an independent adult, and to become the person you really want to be.

Being a teenager isn't easy, and if you've also spent time in care you may feel that you've had more than your fair share of difficult experiences. Hopefully you've also had people to help and support you. It's important that you think about the different choices you can make and the effect these will have on your life, so you can get the best out of your future. As you move from being a teenager into adulthood, you have the right to receive help and support to make good choices.

How to use this book

Only you can make sure you get to where you really want to go in life. Your local authority can give you the support to point you in the right direction. People like teachers, social workers, carers and Connexions Advisers will give you advice to help you along the way. But you are the one becoming the adult and only you can decide how to use the help and support that is offered to you. This is an exciting time in your life, but it may feel a bit scary too – that's why you need to plan ahead.

Think of this book as a bit like a map. When you first take a journey you need to know the names of the different roads and the different places to look out for, otherwise you may get a bit lost and have problems reaching your destination. So you may need to spend a bit of time reading the map. But if you do the journey several times you will find that you learn the way by yourself. You probably won't need the map every time. But it may be useful to have it in your bag or your pocket so you can check it when you need to. So treat this book as a travel companion, a mate you can call upon when you need to.

And whatever you do, remember that no journey worth making is ever straightforward. Maybe you'll take a few wrong turns or find that someone has put a "diversion" sign in the middle of your road. But no matter what has gone wrong before, you don't have to give up or turn back. You can take control of your life and move on. The best travellers are those who learn from their mistakes, check the signs and set off in a new direction.

What you can expect

If you are a young person leaving care, you are entitled to some services and your local authority should make sure that you continue to receive support. The law in England and Wales says that, if you are between the ages of 16 and 21, you should be 'prepared for ceasing to be looked after' (ceasing is another word for ending or finishing). Similar laws are being introduced in Scotland and Northern Ireland. Your local authority must 'advise, assist and befriend' you in order to promote your welfare in the future.

Getting help

Your Personal Adviser

The Children (Leaving Care) Act 2000 says that your local authority should provide you with a Personal Adviser. This person is responsible for assessing your needs (which means working out the kind of support you would need) and deciding what advice, help and support they should give you to help you prepare for the future. As part of this, your Personal Adviser will work with you to prepare a Pathway Plan.

Your Pathway Plan will map out what your needs are and how they will be met. It will include where you are going to live and your plans for education or training or getting a job. The Plan will also say when the local authority thinks you will no longer need support from them or your Personal Adviser.

Your Personal Adviser will also know about grants and financial support that will help you when you are setting up your home or need things for college or your job. They will apply for these on your behalf.

Your local authority also has some financial responsibility for you. You can get extra help with a number of things which are listed later on in this guide. You can always ask your Personal Adviser who will tell you what they are, explain what you can and can't get, and help get the payments for you.

Connexions

Connexions is a government service for all young people aged 13–19, living in England. Each young person has their own Connexions Adviser. This person is usually introduced to them at school or through colleges or drop-in services.

Your Connexions Adviser gives you advice to help you make the journey into adulthood and working life. Connexions works with other organisations to make sure you have a range of opportunities to choose from when you are planning for your future. They can also give you help and advice about issues such as drug abuse, sexual health and homelessness – if you need this. Your Connexions Adviser can also help you identify problems which are stopping you from getting the best out of your education or training. They can put you in touch with special support services who can give you the extra help you need.

Mentors

Some young people leaving care receive help from a mentor. If you think this is something that would help you, you should ask your Personal Adviser or Connexions Adviser if you are "eligible". ("Eligible" means that you fit the rules used to decide if somebody should receive a benefit or service.)

A mentor is someone who:

● **Gets to know you as an individual**

● **Spends a couple of hours with you each week (or fortnight)**

● **Is there for you – you get one-to-one time with your mentor**

● **Listens and doesn't judge you**

● **Is a volunteer**

● **Isn't part of social services, so what they know about you is what you choose to tell them**

Many mentors for young people leaving care are recruited by the Prince's Trust. The Prince's Trust forms partnerships with local organisations who train and supervise mentors who are paired up with local young people leaving care.

Mentors can help you in lots of ways. They can:

- **Give you individual time and attention**
- **Give you advice and encouragement**
- **Provide opportunities for you to learn new skills**
- **Help you find other sources of support**
- **Help you increase your self-esteem and self-confidence**
- **Make you feel that someone is there for you, so you feel less isolated**
- **Help you access grants and programmes provided by the Prince's Trust**

Getting Sorted and *Getting More Sorted*

This guide gives you some tips on moving into your own place, further education, work, managing your money, and other things besides. Obviously, it can only give you a little bit of information, but it does tell you where to go and find out more. There is another book which is like a companion guide to this one, called *Getting Sorted*. It does cover some of the information in this book, but also discusses other things, like how to look after your clothes, clean your home, how to prepare meals, and many other things.

We hope that these books will help you get to where you want to be.

1

Your home

Deciding where to live

IN THIS SECTION:

Deciding where to live

Of course you'd love a huge flat with a Jacuzzi and plasma screen TV! Who wouldn't? But try to stay real and make the best of the options available. You don't want to spend so much on where you live that you can never afford to go out or see your friends. Discuss the options with your Personal Adviser. Give yourself plenty of time to think.

You need to ask yourself these questions:

- **What do I want to do, e.g. go to college or get a job?**

- **How much can I afford?**

- **Do I want to live alone or with other people?**

- **Do I want to live close to family and friends?**

There are many options, for example:

- **Perhaps staying with your foster carers (some young people rent rooms and become "lodgers" in their carer's homes)**

- **Renting a bedsit, flat or house from a private landlord**

- **Renting from a Housing Association**

- **Renting from the council**

- **Being a lodger in someone's house**

- **Staying in bed and breakfast accommodation**

- **Living in a housing co-operative**

- **Living in a mobile home in a trailer park**

- **Going to live with your birth family**

- **Getting a job where accommodation is provided**

- **Staying in a hostel**

- **Staying with friends**

Talk to your foster carers, social worker, Personal Adviser, Connexions Adviser and any other adults who can help you decide what will be best for you, how to plan this and what financial support may be available.

HELPFUL HINT

Ask other people about their experiences of finding somewhere to live. How much do they pay in bills and rent? Do they have any advice about choosing a place to live?

THINK CAREFULLY – WHAT DO YOU NEED IN ORDER TO BE HAPPY AND SECURE WHEN YOU ARE AT HOME?

Useful organisations

www.Connexions.gov.uk – a website for 13–19-year-olds which offers information and advice for making decisions and choices in your life, including: housing, careers, work, learning and money.

You can also contact Connexions Direct advisers by phone on 0808 001 3219, by text on 0776 641 3219, by Textphone on 0800 096 8336 or by email through the website.

www.Housemate.org.uk – this website looks at young people and housing and homelessness.

Shelter has a 24-hour national housing advice service on freephone: 0808 800 4444. For housing in your country, visit www.Shelter.org.uk
www.ShelterCymru.org.uk is a website about housing and homelessness for young people living in Wales.

The Citizen's Advice Bureau website, www.citizensadvice.org.uk has advice on a range of things like housing, education, employment and civil rights. It has different sections for people living in England, Northern Ireland, Scotland and Wales.

For information about mentors and other Prince's Trust projects you can visit **www.Princes-Trust.org.uk**
or email
info@Princes-Trust.org.uk
or phone 020 7543 1234
or freephone 0800 842842

Preparing to move in

IN THIS SECTION:

This is a very practical chapter to help you prepare for the move into your new home. There's a lot to think about and it's a good idea to make some lists of the things you will need.

Although you may be looking forward to the move, having a home of your own can feel a bit scary. Living alone for the first time is a big step for everyone. You should talk to your social worker, foster carer or Personal Adviser if you are worried about anything.

Planning for your move

It's a good idea to start collecting the items you will need in your new home. Here are some basic things. You may think of others which are important for you.

- **Of course, your clothes, music, and other personal stuff!**
- **Toothbrush, soap, shampoo and other such items**
- **Essential household items like toilet rolls, dish cloth and washing up liquid**
- **A first aid kit**
- **A sewing/repair kit**
- **Basic DIY kit**
- **Light bulbs**
- **An address and phone book with essential numbers and a list of emergency phone numbers**
- **Recipes and cookery books**
- **A hot water bottle (great if you're feeling ill or the heating isn't working)**

How to get furniture and equipment

As part of your Pathway Plan, your Personal Adviser will help you organise the furniture and equipment you will need in your new home if you are moving into unfurnished property. They can tell you about any grants you may be eligible for to help you buy the items you need. These may include a Leaving Care Grant, a Decoration Grant or a Community Care Grant. To start with, you only need to get essential items. You also need to work out how much money you have to spend on these things. Luxury items can be added later when you are able to save up for them.

Buying everything new costs a lot of money. If you only have new things then you may not be able to buy very much. If you use your imagination and look around, you can end up with lots of different and interesting things for your new home.

Here are some places where you can buy items cheaply and some things to look out for:

● **Second-hand furniture stores**

● **Car boot sales**

● **Charity shops**

● **Furniture projects (for people on a low income)**

● **Auctions (the everyday ones, not the antique ones)**

● **Self-assembly kits from cut-price stores**

● **Unwanted items from friends/family**

● **"For sale" advertisements in local newspapers/boards in supermarkets and newsagents**

● **Special offers in supermarkets – especially their own brands**

HELPFUL HINT

Have you thought about "customising" your own furniture? You can pick up cheap second-hand items and paint, cover and decorate them so they are unique to you. It's a great way of expressing your own tastes and ideas.

Choosing your furniture

To help you decide what you really need, think about each room in the house. What is essential? Are some pieces of furniture or things like plates and cooking equipment already provided? Don't forget the size of the rooms – don't buy a sofa so big that it won't fit in your home! A tape measure will be useful when viewing your home/your room before you move in.

Kitchen essentials: checklist
- Cooker
- Microwave (only essential if there's no cooker)
- Fridge
- Kettle
- Toaster
- Large saucepan and small saucepan
- Large wooden spoon to stir food while cooking
- Frying pan or wok
- Spatula (that's a "slice" for lifting hot food out of frying pans)
- Sieve or colander for draining water
- 2 plates
- 2 bowls
- 2 sets of cutlery (knife/fork/spoon)
- Mugs
- Sharp knife for chopping and peeling
- Tin opener
- Casserole dish with lid
- Mixing bowl
- Kitchen gloves
- Tea towels

Bedroom essentials: checklist
- Bed
- Duvet
- Duvet cover (2 if possible)
- Bottom sheet (2 if possible)
- Pillows
- Pillow covers (2 if possible)
- Wardrobe or hanging rail
- Chest of drawers or shelf unit
- Computer table or desk (if you are working in your bedroom)

Lounge/living room essentials: checklist
- Comfy chair or beanbag
- Table for eating on and putting drinks on
- Shelf unit

Bathroom essentials: checklist
- [ ] Bath mat
- [ ] Large bath towel (2 if possible)
- [ ] Hand towel (2 if possible)

Other useful items
- [ ] Lamps – you might need one for your bedside or your desk
- [ ] Cushions – useful for making things more cosy
- [ ] Throws – a brightly coloured throw (like a blanket) can transform a dull or shabby armchair
- [ ] A blanket – especially if you've got a lightweight duvet

Nice but not essential
Any grants you receive won't provide these things so you'll have to save up for them.
- [ ] Alarm clock
- [ ] TV
- [ ] TV stand
- [ ] DVD player
- [ ] DVD storage racks
- [ ] Music system
- [ ] CD storage racks
- [ ] Computer

You may already have a computer, or you may need one for your education or work. Having a computer may be part of your Pathway Plan. If you don't have one and feel that you really need one for studying or work (not just for playing games on!) ask about grants that may be available.

Remember that computers are delicate things. Do you still have the box it came in? If not, how will you carry it to prevent it getting shaken up? Will you remember how to plug it in after the move? It may be worth making some notes or doing a drawing of what plugs in where.

➡ RAJ'S STORY

My friend said he had these manky old armchairs and did we want them. I was like, no way! But my sister said I was daft. She said we couldn't afford new chairs so we should take them. She got these blankets from down the market. She dyed them this deep gold colour, and did these funky handprint designs in gold and red. She's good at that stuff. Some of the red paint came off on my mate's jeans when it was first done but Meera found this other paint which is better for chairs. So she did some more blankets and we put the old blankets on the wall instead.

Security

Think about this before you move into your new home – you don't want to move all of your stuff and then have it stolen! Make sure there are secure locks on the doors and windows, give a spare set of keys to someone you trust like a close friend or relative, and don't keep a key under the doormat! You should also start paying insurance for your belongings, generally called Home Contents insurance, which will help you to get replacements if your belongings are stolen or damaged in a flood or fire.

Moving in

You've found your new place, you've got the furniture and things you need, and now it's time to move. This chapter will help you plan for the big day.

Arranging the move

Don't move in a muddle.

- Get a set date for the move and make sure your landlord, housing officer or letting agency agrees to this.

- Do you need to pick up a key before the move?

- Give yourself enough time – moving always takes longer than you think.

- Do you have lots to move? If so, you may need to book a removal van. If you have only a few things, will your foster carers or friends drive you?

- Ask friends to help on the day – extra hands are always useful.

- Start collecting boxes and crates. A removal company will lend you crates but you can ask market stalls and supermarkets for their spare cardboard boxes.

- Start packing in good time and label the boxes, e.g. kitchen, bathroom, bedroom – it will make unpacking easier!

- Keep important items like your phone, some clothes and toiletries (toothpaste, soap, etc) somewhere you can find them easily. You may be too tired to unpack everything on the first night.

> **HELPFUL HINT**
> On the day of the move make sure you have some tea and coffee, a kettle and mugs to hand. And buy a pint of milk and some biscuits. People helping you move will appreciate the offer of a hot drink.

Finding out the how's and where's

Before you move into your new home there are some practical things you need to find out. You can do this by contacting your landlord or housing officer, or asking your new housemates.

- **How is the water heated? Do you get instant hot water or do you need to put an immersion switch on and wait for it to heat up?**

- **How do you pay for the electricity and gas? Will you get a bill from the gas company or is there a "pay-as-you-go" system? If you have a gas or electricity card, where do you get it topped up?**

- **Where do you store your food? If you are sharing a house, do you have your own cupboards and a shelf in the fridge?**

- **Whom do you contact if something doesn't work or goes wrong, e.g. if the heating breaks down, the power goes off or a window gets broken?**

- **How do you turn off the water supply in an emergency?**

- **What do you do if your key is lost or stolen, or you get locked out?**

- **Is there a fire escape? How do you get out of the building if there's a fire?**

- **Is there a smoke alarm? Are there fire extinguishers?**

- **Where is the nearest shop/bank/post office?**

Planning your first night

It can feel strange – even a bit frightening – spending your first night in a new place. In order to help you settle in and feel comfortable, here are some ideas.

- **Make sure you have some food and drink to hand.**

- **Make sure you have some of your favourite belongings around you.**

- **If you have a telephone/mobile phone, make sure it is connected/you have some credit, so you can call someone for a chat.**

- Arrange for a friend to pop around to help you settle in.
- Make sure you have your bed made up and ready to sleep in.
- Set up your music system/TV for a bit of "company".

Living with others

IN THIS SECTION:

You might like to play your music very loudly, invite lots of people around or watch certain programmes on TV. But maybe your foster carers or housemates won't. Small things can turn into big bust-ups if you don't learn to think about other people around you. Compromise is the name of the game when you are living with other people. This means that sometimes you get the things *you* want and sometimes other people get the things *they* want. It's much easier to live in a place where people get along. Don't let a row over whose turn it is to buy a pint of milk turn into World War III.

Many shared houses have some agreed responsibilities (they may be called "house rules") to help everyone live together. If there aren't any, perhaps you could suggest that it might be useful to have some simple ones that everyone discusses and agrees to.

Things to find out in a shared house

These are the kinds of things you need to find out:

- **Is there a cleaning rota?**
- **Who buys cleaning products and toilet rolls?**
- **Do you buy your own food? Do you share things like milk, tea and coffee?**
- **Does everyone cook together or separately?**
- **Do you share the bills and who is in charge of paying them?**
- **Which day does the council collect the rubbish? Who puts the bin bags out for collection?**
- **What about guests and parties? Are they allowed?**
- **What about smoking? Are people allowed to smoke in the house? Remember – it's bad for you!**

How to be an OK person to live with

- **Make sure you do your share of the cleaning and do your washing up – don't leave dirty plates and cups around.**
- **Make sure you have the money ready to pay your share of the bills.**

- Don't leave your things all over shared areas of the house. Tidy up!

- Think about other people before you play your music loudly. Maybe they are trying to sleep or study.

- Think about other people before you invite friends around or organise a party, especially if it's late in the evening. Tidy up afterwards.

- Make sure you lock doors and windows when you go out.

- Knock on other people's bedroom doors before entering.

- If you use up the last of the milk, tea or toilet roll, make sure you replace it.

HELPFUL HINT

It's important to pay your bills for things like gas, electricity and telephones. If you don't pay on time your service may be cut off. There is usually a charge to reconnect the service. You may also be "blacklisted" by credit companies if you run up debts for services.

Be a good negotiator

Negotiation is a very useful skill to develop, especially when you are living with other people. Being a good negotiator means being able to put your point across and listen to what other people think and feel without things turning into an argument.

Here are some ways to be a good negotiator:

- Suggest everyone sits down to talk about the issue.

- Listen carefully to what other people have to say.

- Don't get personal, slag other people off or swear at them.

- Calmly put your point across – don't raise your voice.

- Think about the way you say things. It's OK to say 'I don't agree with you' or 'That's not the way I see it'. It's not OK to say 'You're so wrong' or 'You're stupid!'

- Look for solutions – don't get bogged down with the problems or whether it's someone's fault. Find a solution everyone can agree on, even if it's not perfect.

- Try hard to stick to the decision the group has made. Don't go off and do your own thing even if you are not keen on the decision.

- It's OK to try out an idea for a week or two and then sit down together again and talk about how things have gone. You might want to change the solution if you can find a better one this time.

➡ MIA'S STORY

When I was younger I was pushed around a lot by other people. These days I know my mind and what I want. I like to live somewhere clean and tidy. I'm fussy about it. When I moved into my new place, the other people there were such scruffs. It made me so mad. I used to tell them I wouldn't put up with it. I wrote a list of rules but no-one followed them. I even got into a fight with one of the girls about it.

My boyfriend told me I was stressing too much. He said I should try and see it from other people's point of view. We had a house meeting and I said what I felt. Other people said what they felt. We came up with some rules everyone said they'd follow. It's not perfect but it works OK. I get less stressed now if someone forgets to wash up.

Getting along with others

One of the best ways to make life easy for yourself is getting on with other people.

If people like you, they will make more effort to help you and be nice to you in return. Even if you don't like someone very much, it's better to try and get along with them – it can save a lot of hassle in the long run.

- Respect other people.

- A friendly smile goes a long way – even if you feel shy inside.

- It's good to say "please" and "thank you". It can make a big difference to the way people see you.

- Watch your language! Swearing makes some people feel uncomfortable.

- Make an effort with people you don't know. They probably feel as awkward as you do.

- If you don't know what to talk about, ask someone about themselves, e.g. 'What are you studying? or 'Those are great shoes. Where did you get them?'

- If you disagree with someone, put your point across calmly.

- Respect other people's right to their opinion, i.e. what they think. Don't "rubbish" their ideas if you don't agree with them. Just explain why you see things differently.

- Don't get into a fight. Agree to disagree, and if necessary walk away. Discuss it again later when you are both calm.

- Try to pick the right moment to say difficult things. Judge the other person's mood. If your housemate's just been dumped by his girlfriend, it's not the best time to tell him that you think his new jeans are naff!

- Don't assume people will be free to talk about something just because you are. Ask them if they have a few minutes to sit down and have a chat.

- Everyone needs privacy sometimes. Respect other people's privacy, and explain if you need some "time out" for yourself.

➡ CLAUDIA'S STORY

I'm a very private person and I need my space. Sharing a room
with this other girl at college almost did my head in. She
seemed like she was really stuck up. We got so we didn't speak
to each other most of the time. But I found her crying one day
and we got chatting. She told me she was missing her friends
and she was so lonely. She said she felt like everyone else was
confident and having a good time. I told her I felt like that too.
We got to be good mates after that. She was a good laugh. We
agreed that if either of us needed some space the other one
would go down to the TV lounge. Or one of us would go out for a
bit.

Taking care of others

If you take care of other people they are more likely to take care of
you. Think about the ways your words and actions affect other people.

● Remember people's birthdays. Even a late card or a quick phone
  call is better than nothing.

● If someone is upset, don't ignore it. Ask if there is anything you
  can do, and next time you see them ask if they are now OK.

● If you haven't seen someone for a while, call round or telephone
  to find out how they are.

● If someone's feeling unwell, ask if there is anything you can get
  them.

● If someone's struggling with something, think about what you
  could do or say to be helpful and encouraging.

● Congratulate other people when they do something well.
  Everyone needs a bit of praise.

● Paying someone a compliment can make their day. They may be
  worried that their new haircut is a disaster and your words will
  make them feel a lot better.

● If you have to tell someone something you know they don't want
  to hear, think how you can say it in a way that won't upset them

too much. 'You're cool but please don't ring me so early in the morning. I'm a lot lazier than you!'

Having a house key

Having a house key is an important responsibility. You need to think about the following things.

- Where are you going to keep your key? On a key ring, on a chain around your neck or attached to a belt loop on your jeans?

- Whose house is the key for? Make sure you ask permission before you invite people around.

- Just because you've got a key doesn't mean you can let yourself into the house when you are supposed to be somewhere else!

Pets

Pets can be good companions and some people get lots of pleasure out of looking after animals. But you need to think carefully about the following things before getting a pet.

- Does your housing contract allow you to keep pets? Some contracts ban pets and if you keep one, you will be "in breach" of your contract. You might lose your home if you do this.

- If pets are allowed, does the contract say what sort of pets? A hamster or goldfish may be allowed but dogs and cats may be banned.

- Are the people you live with happy for you to have a pet? Will they help you to look after it?

- Are you sure you will be able to give a pet the care and time it will need?

- Do you have enough space to keep your pet? Even animals like rabbits and guinea pigs need room to run around.

- How much will it cost to buy your pet? Some people re-home cats and dogs from animal rescue centres, but the centre will expect you to show that you can provide a safe, secure home for the animal.

● How much will it cost to look after your pet, e.g. buying food, bedding, cleaning kit, housing? Some pets need annual vaccinations to protect them from diseases.

● What happens if your pet gets ill or is run over? Can you afford vet bills? Some people take out insurance to cover these.

● Who will look after your pet if you are ill or away?

Useful organisations

The RSPCA's website **www.rspca.org.uk** gives advice on caring for different types of pets.

www.allaboutpets.org – the national pet care information service is run by The Blue Cross.

www.bluecross.org.uk – The Blue Cross runs four animal hospitals which give free veterinary care to pets of people on low incomes (although a donation is always appreciated). These hospitals are only in certain parts of the country.

What to do in an emergency

IN THIS SECTION:

In an emergency, don't panic! Stay calm and do something sensible. This chapter will tell you what and how.

Hopefully you won't have to deal with an emergency, but if you do the best thing is to be prepared. If you know where things like fire escapes are, and where to turn the water off, then it's a lot easier to find them in an emergency.

REMEMBER – WHAT YOU DO IN AN EMERGENCY COULD SAVE SOMEONE'S LIFE!

Making emergency phone calls

If you need to call for the **POLICE, AMBULANCE**, or **FIRE BRIGADE in an EMERGENCY...**

DIAL 999

Don't use this number unless it's a real emergency (otherwise the line gets blocked up with calls that aren't urgent, which means someone might die because help doesn't get to them in time).

Emergency	Not an emergency
Someone has fallen down the stairs and is unconscious	You've got a nasty dose of 'flu (call the doctor)
There's a violent fight going on and people are using knives	You noticed someone a bit suspicious hanging round the corner shop (phone the local police)
The house is on fire	You set fire to a chip pan but put it out safely using a fire blanket (read the section on fire blankets)

What you need to do when you dial 999:

1   When you dial 999 the person who answers will ask you which emergency service you require (this means fire, police or ambulance). Think carefully. What is the problem and who do you need? It is vital that you get this right.

2   You will also be asked where you are. If you are at someone's house or in a building, you need to give the address. If you are outside, then give the name of the road you are in. Think of the best way to describe where you are and any landmarks that will

help someone else find you, such as big buildings, parks or supermarkets close by, e.g. 'We are halfway along North Street – opposite the library'.

3 The person on the phone will tell you how long it will be before the emergency service gets to you. Stay where you are and keep calm.

4 If the person on the phone asks you to do something, listen carefully and do exactly as they say. If you are not sure, check again what they want you to do. If necessary, write down the instructions.

HELPFUL HINT

If someone is badly hurt it's usually better not to move them because you may cause them more injury. Try to get advice from 999 first. However, there may be times when you have no choice because you must move them to safety, e.g. there's a fire or they're in a vehicle that might blow up.

 ## LEE'S STORY

You think it's never going to happen – then it does. It was just me and Angie in the house. She was in the kitchen and I heard her screaming and screaming. When I got in there she'd cut her hand right down to the bone – she'd somehow slipped with this carving knife in her hand. I just stood there for a moment and watched the blood going everywhere. Then I got this towel and wrapped it round her hand as tight as I could. And I rang 999. The woman I spoke to told me how to wrap her hand properly to stop the bleeding. They told me how to keep Angie a bit calmer until the ambulance arrived. It was brilliant having that person to help me.

Fire exits and plans

THE MOST IMPORTANT THING TO DO IN A FIRE IS TO GET OUT OF THE BUILDING.

It is very important you know how to get out of your house if there is a fire. Some buildings have fire escapes which take you out through a special door or staircase, but most ordinary houses don't, so you need to work out your own fire escape plan.

You need to think about:

1 **How many different ways are there to get out of your home? Think about where the doors and windows lead to and where the staircases are.**

2 **How would you get out if you were trapped upstairs?**

3 **How would you get out if you were trapped downstairs?**

4 **Are there any windows that lead on to flat roofs, or which are close enough to the ground that you could use in an emergency?**

5 **If any of these windows are locked, can you unlock them or get to the key easily?**

HELPFUL HINT

Once you have worked out your escape routes, write them down or draw them clearly on a piece of paper. Pin this somewhere where everyone can see it.

Using fire extinguishers

There are different coloured fire extinguishers for different types of fires. In your home you should have at least one **fire extinguisher upstairs** (usually on the landing) and one **downstairs** (usually in the kitchen). You should also have a fire blanket kept near the cooker.

The best type of fire extinguishers to have at home are **powder** filled ones because they can be used on most types of fires.

Types of fire extinguishers

These are the different types of fire extinguishers that you can get to use on different kinds of fires.

IT IS IMPORTANT THAT THE RIGHT KIND OF FIRE EXTINGUISHER IS USED ON THE RIGHT KIND OF FIRE OR IT CAN MAKE THE FIRE WORSE!

DRY CHEMICAL/ POWDER HALON Multi purpose

WATER wood and paper

CARBON DIOXIDE liquids and electrical

A POWDER FIRE EXTINGUISHER CAN BE USED ON ALL TYPES OF FIRES.

HELPFUL HINT

FIRE EXTINGUISHERS ARE NOT TOYS AND SHOULD NEVER BE PLAYED WITH. Playing with a fire extinguisher could damage it and then it would not work if it was needed in a fire. Someone could die because of this.

How to use a fire extinguisher

USE UPRIGHT PULL OUT SAFETY CLIP

STAND BACK 2 METRES AIM AT THE BASE

SQUEEZE THE LEVER AND SWEEP FROM SIDE TO SIDE OF THE FIRE

Using a fire blanket

Every kitchen should have a fire blanket in it somewhere near the cooker. (If you don't have one, ask your landlord about this.)

Fire blankets are designed to be used on cooking fires, such as when a chip pan or toaster catches alight.

- **Fire blankets are good to use on flat pan fires on the cooker or for wrapping around someone whose clothes are on fire.**

- **They are ideal to keep in the kitchen, but they are also good for use in other parts of the house.**

- **Make sure your fire blanket conforms to (meets) British Standard BS 6565.* There will be a symbol which tells you this on the outside.**

*All equipment that you buy should meet what is called "British Standards". This means that they have been tested to make sure that they are safe and that they work properly. If something you buy, such as electrical equipment or toys, does not have the British Standards symbol on them, it means they may not be safe and should not be used.

What to do in a power cut

A power cut is when the lights and other electric things – like toasters, cooker, microwaves – stop working because the electricity supply has "cut out" or has been cut off by the power station.

Make sure you have a torch in the house, and remember where it is, so you can find it if the lights go off.

1 **If the power goes off the most common reason is because the *trip switch* has flicked off. The *trip switch* can be found in the *fuse box*, which is the place where all the fuses for the electrics in the house are kept.**

2 ***Fuse boxes* are usually found in the hallway, utility room, garage or cupboard under the stairs.**

3 **The *trip switch* is the switch that says whether the power is *on* or *off*. When you flick this switch to ON the power should come back on. If it doesn't then you will need to call a qualified electrician.**

4   The *trip switch* will flick off for a number of reasons, but the most common one is that too many sockets and lights are on in the house, so you may need to turn some things off before you can reset the *trip switch*.

5   Very rarely, the power supply may be cut off by the electricity company. This could be for safety or for maintenance reasons and will not last for long.

NEVER ATTEMPT TO REPAIR ELECTRICS YOURSELF UNLESS YOU ARE TRAINED. THE AMOUNT OF POWER RUNNING THROUGH THE MAINS COULD ELECTROCUTE YOU!

How to turn the water off

If you have a burst pipe (usually when they freeze in winter) or discover any pipe leaking you will need to turn the water off until you can get it repaired.

1   When you first move into a house or flat make sure you know where the *stopcock* is. The stopcock is a kind of tap which turns the water on or off. It is usually under the kitchen sink or in the kitchen somewhere, but in old houses it could be almost anywhere!

2   Use the *stopcock* to turn the water off.

3   When you have turned the water off, run all the taps until no water is coming out to empty the system of water.

4   Remember to turn off the central heating, as there will be no water in the radiators to heat them. If you don't you will seriously damage or break the heating system.

> **HELPFUL HINT**
>
> When the water is back on remember to turn the taps on slowly as the water will burst from the taps and could damage the system.

First aid kits

You should have a basic first aid kit in the house which can be used for minor accidents and injuries, such as small cuts and bruises, and minor insect bites.

You can buy this from most chemists and some supermarkets.

What you need in a first aid kit

A first aid kit (for one person) should have in it:

- **2 triangular bandages (size 96cm x 96cm)**
- **a large dressing (18cm x 18cm)**
- **10 assorted plasters**
- **6 safety pins**
- **2 non-alcoholic wipes**
- **a pair of latex gloves**

You can also include:

- **antiseptic cream/liquid/lotion**
- **cotton wool**
- **any other items you may need if you have a medical condition**

Make sure that you replace anything you use from the first aid kit, so that you have everything you need next time.

HELPFUL HINT

How much do you know about first aid? Organisations like St John's Ambulance run first aid courses all over the UK. For information about a first aid course in your area look on their website at www.sja.org.uk. This website also has downloadable fact sheets on first aid.

Emergency contact numbers

It is a good idea to keep a list of emergency contact numbers somewhere noticeable so that you – or someone else – can find it in a hurry.

This list should include phone numbers for:

- **Your local police station**

- **Your doctor**

- **Any other medical person you might need in an emergency, e.g. your specialist**

- **A close friend/carer/family member (it's a good idea to let these people know that they are on your emergency list)**

- **Your social worker or key worker**

- **A plumber**

- **An electrician**

- **The gas board**

Telephones

IN THIS SECTION:

Many people own mobile phones and some people also have a "landline" phone in their home. Phones are a great way of keeping in touch with friends, finding out information and making appointments. But you also need to think about the cost of buying and using a phone and whether you can afford the bill.

Save money by thinking about whether your call or text is absolutely necessary. Could it wait until another time? Will you be seeing the person you are contacting soon so that you can talk to them face-to-face?

What kind of phone?

You need to think about what kind of phone is best for you, a landline, a mobile phone, or both.

- **Do you need to make or receive calls while you are out and about? For example, do you have a job where a phone is important for getting updates from your employer about where your next job will be? Or do you need to be able to call for assistance, for example, if you sometimes need urgent help because of a medical condition?**

- **Landlines are usually cheaper to use than mobiles but they come with certain fixed responsibilities. Is there a landline already installed in your home? If not, how much will it cost to install one once the cost is divided amongst everyone in the house?**

- **How much will it cost to get an existing landline in the house re-connected once the cost is divided among everyone who lives there?**

- **How will you split the bill between everyone who lives there?**

- **Are you less likely to make unnecessary calls if you have a telephone only in the house and not in your pocket?**

- **Will you feel safer or more secure if you have a phone you can carry around with you?**

How to get a landline

Your landlord should tell you whether there is a landline in your home and whether it's connected.

If there isn't a landline already, or if there is one that needs re-connecting (and your landlord gives permission for this), you need to follow the steps below.

If you are under 16, you will need to ask your landlord if they will set the line up on your behalf.

To get an existing landline reconnected

● **Find the telephone number for the company who provided the phone, in the phone directory or via the internet. Call the number for getting lines reconnected.**

Follow steps 3–4 below of *To get a new landline installed*. In most cases the company just "switches" the line back on and an engineer will not need to call.

 MAX'S STORY

When I moved in they had this house phone line. I wasn't planning on using it but it seemed like everyone paid a bit of the bill. I wasn't keen on that, but then I had to make all these calls to people down south to try and set up the gig for our band. I don't use my mobile much during the day and it's well expensive to make those kind of calls. One of the lads in the house said you should use the landline. So I did. And he was right. It was cheaper.

To get a new landline installed

1   Ask around and look on the internet to find out the best phone deal for you. Most people think of BT (British Telecommunications) but there are other phone companies which supply landlines.

2   Find the telephone number of the phone company you want via the internet or a telephone directory. Ask if you can borrow

someone's phone, or use a phone box, and call the number for installations.

3   You will be given several options to help you get through to the right person and service you need. You may be asked to choose the option you want by selecting the number that relates to this, e.g. 'choose 1 for connections, choose 2 for queries about your bill' and so on. You may be asked to press this number on the phone keypad. Sometimes you may be asked to say this number into the phone. You will need to speak very clearly.

4   Once you are through to someone, they will probably ask you another set of questions in order to get the details they need to have the line installed. This may include your address, bank account details, age, etc.

5   Once you have given all the correct information, the phone company will arrange for an engineer to call. They will usually tell you on which day and whether this will be in the morning or the afternoon, but not exactly what time.

6   Once a convenient date has been arranged, you need to make sure that you or someone else is at home to let the engineer in.

7   Write down a note of the phone company's number and any other details you need, for example, the name of the person you spoke to. Keep this somewhere you can find it easily.

8   Ask to see the engineer's ID card before you let them in the house. If you feel uncomfortable or you're not sure this person is who they say they are, say you are sorry but you need to arrange another time. Contact the phone company straight away and explain the problem. Arrange another time and maybe ask for a friend or someone you trust to be with you.

HELPFUL HINT

When you arrange for a landline to be installed, you are paying for the connection to the service and for rental of the phone line. Some people rent phones from the phone company but many people buy their own phone. You plug your own phone into the socket the phone company provides.

Not all landline phones look like "landlines" – some look and feel a bit like mobiles. They are portable phones which sit in a charger which is connected to the landline. This means you can carry them from room to room, but you have to put them back in the charger after you have finished or they will run out of power.

Using the phone effectively

You're probably the expert on chatting to your friends on the phone but when it comes to calling people about training, jobs, doctor's appointments, etc, you need to follow some basic rules. Often the phone will be answered by someone on a switchboard.

● **Be polite and friendly.**

● **Say at the beginning who you want to speak to – 'Hello, please may I speak to…'**

● **Be prepared to say who you are. Some receptionists won't put your call through unless they know who is calling.**

● **If the person isn't there, ask if you can leave a message. Give your name and phone number and a brief description of why you want to speak to them, e.g. 'I'd like to ask a few questions about the training course you are advertising'.**

● **If the receptionist asks questions you don't want to answer say 'It's OK – I'll call back another time'.**

● **Always say 'Thank you' before you disconnect.**

Leaving messages

If you need to leave a message for someone on an answerphone:

1 Say who you are (give your family name as well as your first name).

2 Say what time and date you are calling.

3 If you want them to call you back, make sure you leave a phone number (or an address or email they can contact you at).

4 Speak slowly and clearly, especially when giving your phone number or your address.

5   If it helps, put the phone down and think about what you want to say. Write it down. When you are clear, ring back.

6   If you make a mistake or forget something important, ring back and leave another message.

Using a pay phone

● Pay phones normally take 10p, 20p, 50p and £1 coins.

● Try to use small coins – 10ps and 20ps – as some pay phones will not give change. Before you put in any larger coins, make sure the person you need to speak to is there and can talk to you for long enough to use up the larger coin.

● Emergency phone numbers are displayed in the phone box. If you cannot find the number you need, ring the cheapest directory enquiry service.

● If you do not have any money, you can still use the phone by making a reverse charge call. This means the person you are ringing will have to accept payment for the call before you are connected. Only do this if it is a very important call as people can get very annoyed about being asked to pay, and even more so if they don't know you!

How to make a reverse charge call

1   Dial 0800 and the word 'reverse' (using the letters on the number buttons).

2   An operator will answer the phone and ask you for the number you want to be connected to. They will then try to connect you. They will ask the person at the other end if they are willing to accept the charges.

HELPFUL HINT

There are lots of directory enquiries numbers to choose from, but they all charge for the call and some are very expensive. Do you know the cheapest ones to use? Also, think about checking in a telephone directory like Yellow Pages. If you have easy access to the internet you can check addresses and telephone numbers online – for free.

Using Yellow Pages

Yellow Pages telephone directories are delivered free to homes. They have everything listed in alphabetical order (that is, from A–Z). For example, B for Builders, D for Dentists, S for Sports Centres.

Yellow Pages is also available on the internet at www.yell.com.

HELPFUL HINT

Sometimes what you are trying to find will be listed under a different name. For example, a carpenter may be listed under 'joiners'. So, if you can't find what you are looking for, think what else it may be called. There is also a list of everything in the back of the book, so you can look down the list until you find what you are after.

Useful organisations

www.consumerdirect.gov.uk provides advice and guidance on your rights as a consumer.

www.citizensadvice.org.uk is run by the Citizens Advice service and has details of your local Citizens Advice Bureaux (England, Wales and Northern Ireland). If you live in Scotland, contact **www.cas.org.uk**.

www.consumercomplaints.org.uk is run by the local Trading Standards Service to help you make complaints. It covers the whole of the UK.

www.yell.com is the online service for Yellow Pages.

Mobiles

IN THIS SECTION:

If you read all the computer and gadget magazines you may not need this chapter. But you might also find some useful advice on what to do if your mobile stops working just after you buy it.

Buying a mobile phone

If you buy a mobile phone there are several things you need to think about. You need to make sure that you get:

- **The right phone for you**
- **The best price**
- **The right contract**
- **The right coverage**

Go to a mobile phone shop which sells phones made by different companies. Tell the sales assistant what sort of phone you are looking for and how you want to use it. Get them to suggest a range of different phones and contracts that will be the best value for you. Some supermarkets also sell phones and it's worth checking what they can offer. You might also find special deals on the internet – but check the contract details very carefully.

Don't rush into a decision. Get plenty of information on the choices available and take it away to look at before you make a decision. Ask friends and people you know who have a mobile.

These are the key things to think about when you buy a mobile:

1 *Coverage* – does the network you want have good coverage in your area? Some phone companies have poor reception in some parts of the country.

2 *Power* – how long will your phone last before it needs recharging? The flashiest looking phone isn't much good if it keeps running out of charge. Compare minimum "talk times" between different phones.

3 *Usability* – is the phone easy to use and comfortable to hold? Flashy phones aren't always the easiest to use.

4 *Doing the right things* – not all phones do the same things in the same way, e.g. some don't save messages, or delete texts if you can't send them straight away. Which services matter most to you?

5 *Don't pay for what you don't need* – do you really need a camera or video phone? If you don't – or if you think the temptation to use it will cost you too much – don't buy one.

6 *Don't pay too much* – prices vary from store to store so shop around. And remember you'll pay over the odds for the latest phones. New phones are launched every few months, so in six months time the phone you really like will probably be cheaper.

7 *The right deal* – pay-as-you-go can be the best deal because you don't have to pay rental. But it can also be more expensive because the calls can cost more than rental deals. (If you are under 18 you will probably be restricted to pay-as-you-go unless a responsible adult is willing to take a contract out for you.)

8 *Are you a heavy texter?* If so, look for deals that allow you to buy text bundles at cheap prices.

If your phone doesn't work

If you have a problem with the mobile you have bought you need to check the following things:

● Check there really is a fault and that the problem is not caused by user error (you using it wrongly), an accident, or just normal wear and tear.

● If possible, collect together all the paperwork for your phone and check the details/instructions before you make the complaint (this can save embarrassment).

● You will need to contact the place where you bought the phone to report the problem and find out what they will do about it.

● If the fault is with the phone, you should contact the shop where you bought it.

● If the fault is with the network or SIM card, you need to contact your service provider (the company which provides the phone service).

LEAH'S STORY

I got offered this phone as a free upgrade. It was dead cute. But I got so I hated it that much I would've thrown it out the window. Where I live there is bad coverage. I'd be, like, halfway through a call and the phone would cut off. So I'd try and send a text but if I was on the bus or something it would go wrong. The text wouldn't go through and it would disappear. It used to make me so mad. I complained several times but they didn't do anything. In the shop they said it wasn't their fault because the phone was made by another company. I should've read the contract properly. In the end I moved to another company when my contract ran out. It's much better. I wouldn't have one of those tiny phones again.

Your rights and your mobile

The law says that if you buy a mobile, it must be:

- of satisfactory quality
- fit for its purpose
- as described in the literature (that's the stuff written in the advertising leaflets)

If you buy a phone and find that it doesn't do some or all of these things, you have rights.

Your rights and the phone

If you have only had the phone a few weeks or haven't had enough time to check it, you are probably entitled to a refund for a fault or because it was poorly described, or you may be able to request a replacement.

If the fault is only minor (something small) and is easily put right, it is reasonable to accept a repair. If this repair is not satisfactory, you should then be able to ask for a replacement or refund.

If you have had the phone longer than a few weeks, you will probably still be entitled to a repair or replacement carried out within a reasonable period of time after you bought it. If this repair is not OK, you should be entitled to a replacement or refund.

If the phone can't be repaired or replaced economically you are entitled to a refund. The trader may make a reduction (take some money away) from the price you paid for the use you have already had from the phone.

If you are out of pocket in any other way, you may be entitled to compensation over and above the price of the phone.

If you are entitled to a replacement or a refund, the trader has to arrange this and can't tell you to go back to the manufacturer.

Your rights and the network

When you buy a phone, you need to be connected to a network in order to use it. You may do this by having a line rental contract or by buying pay-as-you-go vouchers. When you take out this contract or buy these vouchers, you are entering into a contract with the "service provider" (the company which provides the connection). If there are problems, you may be entitled to a refund or compensation.

You need to remember the following things.

● **Always read the terms and conditions of your contract carefully.**

● **You usually have seven working days to cancel a contract if you do change your mind (but not always – check this carefully). After that time you have no right to cancel the service simply because you change your mind.**

● **If you choose a contract phone rather than a pay-as-you-go-phone, you will be committed to using a certain network, at a certain tariff (rate), for a minimum length of time.**

● **You have no rights to repairs, refunds or replacements if you have not used or looked after your phone in line with any instructions, e.g. if you drop it in the bath you won't get it replaced by the shop!**

● **Wear and tear caused by your use of the phone is not counted as a fault. If you get dust or water in the phone, or jam the keys by pressing them too hard, that is your problem.**

● **Your rights cannot be taken away by terms and conditions written into a notice, receipt, contract, warranty or guarantee.**

Unfortunately, it's all a bit complicated! If you are having problems understanding your rights or getting a shop to replace faulty goods, it's best to get help. Consumer organisations like the Citizens Advice Bureau can help you.

The internet

IN THIS SECTION:

Using the internet

What can you use the internet for?

Email

● **Contacting friends and family**

● **Contacting your tutor, social worker, Personal Adviser or Connexions Adviser**

● **Contacting someone from an organisation whose services you might use**

Internet

● **Finding information and advice**

● **Buying stuff**

● **Fun and entertainment**

You may have an internet connection at home. If you don't, you can often use the internet at these places:

● **Your local library**

● **A local voluntary organisation**

● **College**

● **An internet café – although there is a charge for use in these**

What you need

To use either email or the internet, you will need access to a computer that has an internet connection. If you do not have a computer, there may be internet-connected computers that you can use in your local library, a local voluntary organisation, college, an internet café (there is a charge for these) or at a friend's place.

If you have a computer and a landline phone, then you could consider getting an internet connection at home, but you need to think carefully about what this will cost. Are there several of you who could club together to pay for this? If you need this for your work or study, there may be a grant to help you with this – talk to your Connexions or career adviser.

There are several different types of internet connection service available:

- **Dial-up services**

- **Broadband services**

- **Cable services**

Dial-up services use your landline phone to connect to the internet. This means that while you are using the internet you won't be able to use your landline phone. These come in two different types of package – "fixed rental charge", where you pay a fixed amount per month however much you use the internet, and "pay per use", where you are charged for the time you spend on the connection.

Broadband services offer a faster connection which means that you can download music and video, but they can be more expensive. They require the phone company to make changes to the way your phone landline works, so you have to take out a longer contract (usually a year).

Cable services are provided by the companies that provide cable TV services. Usually they offer deals if you sign up for their TV, phone and internet connections together.

The different types of services and costs can be very confusing and it is best to ask someone before you start to pay for something.

- **Ask a friend who knows about computers.**

- **Ask at college or the people who run the computer department where you work.**

- **Read computer magazines – these may confuse you at first but keep reading and you'll soon pick it up.**

- **Check out a local computer users group – they are usually very happy to help.**

- **Or why not attend a computer course? Your Connexions Adviser or school or college should be able to sort this out for you.**

Email

To use email you need a way of getting onto the internet and a way of sending, reading and replying to messages.

If you have your own computer then you can use an email program to do this or a web-based email service.

If you have to use a computer somewhere else, then you will have to use a web-based service such as Hotmail or Yahoo, but there are also many others. There are advantages to using a web-based email service:

● **You can access it anywhere there are computers connected to the internet.**

● **The services are usually free.**

● **They're quite easy to sign up for.**

● **They can be helpful if you're going away and need to keep in contact with someone.**

Email DOs and DON'Ts

Do

● **Keep email messages as short as possible.**

● **Think about who you are sending to – what you send to your mates is one thing, but a lot of people use email just like letters and expect things to be clear and well written.**

● **Check your spelling and don't use lots of jargon, especially if you are contacting strangers or asking people for help.**

● **Read the message and make sure it says what you mean before you send it.**

Don't

● **Send nasty messages to people who have turned you down for something.**

● **Pass on hoax messages.**

● **Use it to harass people.**

Exploring on the Web

The Web (or World Wide Web) is what most people mean when they say "the internet". It's a series of connected websites (millions and millions of them). Websites have addresses which you type into the address bar of your internet browser. For example, the Connexions website address is www.connexions.gov.uk.

You can use the Web for:

- **Looking up information**

- **Help with your college work**

- **Checking train times**

- **Finding out information from all over the world**

- **Checking your bank or building society account**

- **Fun – you can download music and videos (be careful if you have a slow connection that you pay for by the minute because a song can take a long time to download)**

- **Buying things, if you have a credit or debit card**

- **Selling things through websites like ebay**

Safety online

The internet is like any other "place". There are people using the internet who want to rip you off and do things that are illegal.

- **If you are looking to buy something from a website, does it have a phone number to call if anything goes wrong? Do you trust the company that runs the site? Look for the secure site symbol.**

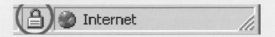

- **Any number of sites offer music for free – in most cases this is illegal. You usually have to pay for music.**

- **Don't give out your contact details unless you really have to – and then only if you trust the people you are giving them to.**

- **Be careful about arranging to meet people you have "met" in chatrooms or on dating sites. You never know who they really are.**

- **Only enter financial or personal details into a website if it has a secure address and "padlock" symbol, which show that it is a secure site.**

● **If something is illegal to buy in the UK, then it's illegal if you buy it from another country over the internet.**

Useful organisations

BBC Webwise – www.bbc.co.uk/webwise/ – gives advice on getting started

UK Online Centres – www.ufi.com/ukol/ – These are public centres where you can learn to use computers and the Internet. Call free on 0800 771 234.

For info on staying safe online visit **www.getsafeonline.org** and **www.thinkuknow.co.uk**.

Children and young people's charity **NCH** produces its own internet safety guide – visit **www.nch.org.uk** to find out more.

Your health

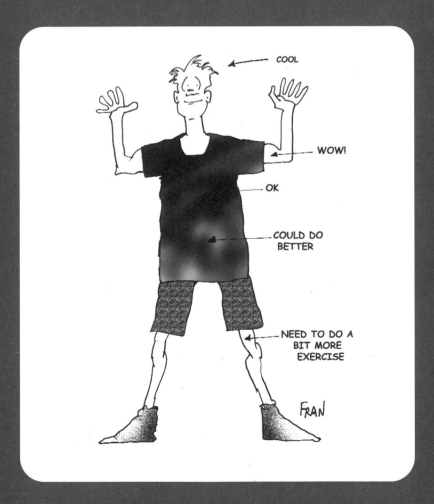

Looking after your health

IN THIS SECTION:

Are older people always going on about how important it is to look after your health? It can be a bit boring to hear this again and again, but health is one of the most important things we have. If you neglect or damage your health you will lose out on many good things. You will also make life a lot harder for yourself. If you visit people in hospital take a look around you – aren't you glad it's not you in the bed with lots of tubes hanging out of you? Keep it that way if you possibly can.

Registering with a GP

Everyone should be registered with a GP (doctor). If you're not, you need to do the following:

1 **Find out where your nearest GP surgeries are.**

2 **Ask around to see if there are surgeries that people recommend.**

3 **Find their phone number in the phone directory or on the internet, or call in and ask if they have a place for you. If they do not have a place, they can put you on a waiting list.**

4 **If you have been put on a waiting list, make sure you know how long it will be before a place comes up. If the list is a long one, keep looking for somewhere else.**

5 **When you find a surgery and they have a place for you, you will be asked to attend a medical with a nurse and complete an application form. The form is used to keep your basic details together, such as your name, address, date of birth and National Insurance number. Make sure you have as much of this information with you as possible. A foster carer may have a carer-held health record about you. If so, you can show this to your GP. It would also be useful for your GP to be told of who your previous GP was, so that they can make sure that they have up-to-date medical records for you. The medical examination at the GP's surgery may include measuring your weight, height and blood pressure. As well as being asked about any health concerns, you will probably be asked whether you smoke or drink and whether you are having a sexual relationship. Everyone who joins a doctor's surgery gets asked these questions.**

If you're under 16 an adult may need to register you.

Health care is provided free through the NHS. You will not be asked to pay to see a doctor or be treated in a hospital, unless you go to a "private" doctor or want treatment that is not paid for by the NHS.

GP surgeries have something called an "out of hours" service for people who are ill when the surgery is not open. **You should only use this if you feel really unwell and you cannot wait until the surgery opens.** Ring the surgery number. There will probably be an answerphone message giving you an emergency number to call, or you may be asked to leave a message and someone will call you back (see Health Emergencies – later in this chapter).

Registering with a dentist

Follow steps 1 to 4 above of registering with a GP.

You will still be asked to give some information/fill in a form but you will not have a "medical". You may get a "check up" instead.

When you register with a dentist it only lasts for 15 months. If you do not go to the dentist during this time your registration may run out.

Dental treatment isn't free in the same way that NHS treatment is free. Some dentists only treat people who can pay for the service. But generally:

- **If you are under 18 you will get free dental treatment**

- **If you are under 19 and in full-time education you will get free dental treatment**

- **People on benefits like Income Support or Job Seekers Allowance get free dental treatment**

- **Other people on low incomes may also be able to get dental treatment more cheaply**

In an emergency (when you can't wait until the dentist's surgery opens) ring the surgery number. There will probably be an answerphone message giving you an emergency number to call, or you may be asked to leave a message and someone will call you back.

If you are not registered with a dentist you can call NHS Direct on 0845 46 47.

HELPFUL HINT

If you are frightened of going to the dentist, tell the dentist this. If the dentist knows you are frightened they can often do things to help you relax. There are also things they can do to make it easier for you, like doing one filling at a time rather than several fillings in one go.

Going to the opticians

Don't neglect your eyesight – If you think that you can't see as well as you should, get your eyes tested.

A list of opticians in your area can be obtained from the Eye Care Trust (0845 129 5001) or local Yellow Pages, etc, and every high street will have a number of opticians shops.

If you do need glasses, the NHS range is cheaper. Remember you don't have to buy your glasses from the optician who tested your eyes, but you will need a copy of your prescription – look around for the best deal. If you choose to have contact lenses you will have to pay for them yourself, so again, shop around and don't forget they are easy to lose, so insure them.

Health emergencies

- **If you or someone else is seriously ill or badly hurt call 999 and ask for an ambulance. (DO NOT CALL 999 UNLESS ABSOLUTELY NECESSARY.)**

- **If you or someone else needs to go to hospital but can get there in a car or taxi, call a taxi or ask someone for a lift.**

- **If you are worried about yourself or someone else, but don't know if you need to go to hospital, call the NHS Direct 24-hour helpline on 0845 46 47. They will ask you for details of the illness or injury and advise you on what you need to do. Sometimes the person you speak to will take some details and get somebody else to call you back.**

- **Many places now have an NHS "walk in" centre run by nurses. You don't need to make an appointment. This can be a good place** to start if someone isn't very well but it isn't so serious that they need to go straight to hospital.

HELPFUL HINT

If someone has taken an overdose, don't wait! Dial 999 straight away. Follow any instructions you are given. Acting quickly can save someone's life.

Getting a prescription

Your doctor may give you a prescription for medicine or for things like asthma inhalers.

You need to do the following:

● Ask where you can get the medicine from. Your GP or the GP's receptionist will be able to tell you where the nearest pharmacy (chemist) is.

● If you are not sure what the prescription is for, ask your GP before you collect it.

● You will be asked at the pharmacy whether you will be paying for your prescription. If you are not sure, on the back of the prescription it tells you who needs to pay and who doesn't. Your pharmacist will also be able to help you with this.

● You may have to wait for your prescription to be made up, so ask how long it will take and either wait or arrange to call back later.

● Some prescriptions can be collected straight from your GP. Your GP should tell you if this is the case.

If you have a medical condition

You may have a medical condition such as diabetes, asthma or eczema. It is important that you understand how to manage your condition, so that you can keep yourself healthy.

This may include:

1   How to keep medications safely, e.g. you may need to keep some medications in the fridge.

2   How to use medications safely, e.g. what dose you need to take and how often you should take it.

3   If you need to inject any medicines or use things like inhalers, make sure you know how to do this safely and effectively. If you haven't done something for a while and can't remember how to do it, ask to be shown again.

4   Make sure you know when to seek help.

Your medical records

Your GP will have notes and records about your medical history. This will include the results of any medical tests and appointments your GP has referred you to, e.g. with a hospital or specialist. Your notes will also contain details of the "diagnosis" (description of symptoms) of any medical condition that you may have. Your GP will be able to tell you more about this.

It is your right to be able to see your medical records, but you will have to make an appointment with your GP. (In some very rare cases a doctor may hold back information if they think it will cause "serious harm" for a person to see part of their medical records.)

Preparing for an appointment

Going to see a doctor, nurse, specialist, or therapist can be worrying, especially if what you are going to talk about is sensitive or personal.

To help you prepare for the appointment:

●   Write down any questions you want to ask before you go

●   Write down any answers you are given when you are there

●   Take someone with you for support if you want to

●   If you don't understand, ask for the information to be explained again

● **Try not to get too embarrassed about things – everyone has to get advice from time to time**

Get wise about drugs

I MEAN APART FROM THE OUTRAGEOUS COST, THE FACT THAT IT WILL MAKE YOU ILL LONG BEFORE IT KILLS YOU, THAT IT CONTROLS YOUR LIFE, RUINS YOUR SKIN, GIVES YOU A COUGH AND MAKES YOU SMELL LIKE AN OLD ASHTRAY *WHAT'S WRONG WITH SMOKING?*

© FRAN

We know you're going 'Oh no – here comes the lecture' but drugs – which include solvents, cigarettes and alcohol – can seriously screw up your life.

Get wise about drugs. Don't believe everything your friends tell you. There are useful websites and helplines where you can get the full facts.

Drugs

People take drugs for a lot of reasons, some medical and some social.

Some drugs are legal, such as alcohol and cigarettes, and some are illegal, such as dope, coke, ecstasy and smack.

Although drugs can make you feel better for a short while, the effects wear off and can leave you feeling anxious, depressed and messed up. In extreme cases drugs can kill.

Other risks include:

● **Getting caught in possession of illegal drugs**

● **Mood swings and being unable to function properly in your daily life**

● **Infections from sharing needles**

● **You can get addicted**

● **Your habit will cost you a lot of money**

● **Risks to your unborn child**

The best advice is – don't start in the first place. But if you have a drugs problem then seek help. Talk to someone you trust, visit your GP or call a confidential helpline. You won't be reported to the police for seeking help.

Solvents

Sniffing solvents is **very dangerous.** You are at risk of:

● **suffocation**

● **poisoning**

● **choking on your vomit**

● **death**

Like any drug, the feeling you get from sniffing solvents soon wears off. You will then feel much worse than you did before.

THE SHORT-TERM EFFECTS ARE NOT WORTH THE RISK AND CAN DO YOU LASTING HARM.

Alcohol

Alcohol is a drug as it stops you from functioning properly. You can also get addicted to it.

A small amount of alcohol in a social situation, such as at a party or when you're out with your mates is fine, but drinking a lot of alcohol can seriously damage your health and prevent you from functioning properly.

Do you know what the recommended "units" of alcohol are for men and women? At the time we wrote this guide it was 14 for women and 21 for men – in a whole week! Do you know that a "unit" is not the same as a glass? Some drinks like spirits and cocktails contain 2 or more units per drink.

The limit doesn't mean that it is healthy or safe to drink that amount every week. To keep really healthy you should try and drink no more than 5–10 units whether you are a man or woman. And try to make sure you have at least one day a week when you don't drink any alcohol.

MEL'S STORY

For my cousin's hen party we planned this mad night. We started with a pub crawl and then hit a club. In the club they were selling doubles of vodka half price. We all had our tongues hanging out, we were that thirsty from dancing. The thing with vodka is that it goes down so easy. I don't remember how I got to the hospital. I do remember that stomach pump thing though. It was disgusting. But the worse thing was I couldn't fly to Spain with everyone the next day. So I missed the wedding. I can't look at vodka now. Just the smell of it makes me throw up.

HELPFUL HINT

It's not OK to "save up" all your units of alcohol for one day. "Binge drinking" is extremely bad for you. You can get alcohol poisoning from drinking too much in one go, which can kill you or cause permanent damage to your brain.

If you think someone has alcohol poisoning – don't wait. Seek urgent medical help.

Smoking

If you smoke you are at risk from:

- lung cancer
- bronchitis
- heart disease
- early death

Reasons for giving up smoking:

- You can never be totally healthy if you smoke – however much you exercise
- Smoking affects the way you perform – true athletes don't smoke

- You spend lots of money you could use for other things

- Your breath smells – so does your hair, your clothes and things like your sheets

- Smoking affects other people's health – they breathe in your smoke (which can seriously harm them)

- Smoking while pregnant can seriously harm your unborn baby

- You run the risk of getting serious illnesses like cancer and heart disease

- Most smokers don't live as long as other people

- If you get a disease caused by smoking your treatment costs the NHS a lot of money. This money could be used to help people who have health problems they didn't cause by smoking!

- Smoking affects so many people. How would you explain to your partner or your child that you are going to die because you have a disease caused by smoking?

Giving up smoking

We know it isn't easy but it's an incredibly worthwhile thing to do. However, unless you really want to give up smoking, you may not succeed. You will need a lot of support if you decide to give up. Call a helpline or go to your GP to find out what help is available.

The best thing to do is:

- Decide on a start date when you are not stressed or under pressure

- Make sure you stick to this date!

- Think about the money you will save and how much healthier you will be

- When you would normally smoke, think about what you will do instead

- If you do have a cigarette, don't give in! Just stop again and keep trying to stay away from cigarettes.

- Take one day at a time. Every day without a cigarette is a success in itself.

Useful organisations

Talk to Frank and **The National Drugs Helpline** offer lots of down-to-earth information and advice about drugs. Call 0800 776 600, or look at www.ndh.org.uk. All help is confidential and they're open 24 hours a day.

Drugscope gives safety advice about drugs. Visit their website at www.drugscope.org.uk.

ADFAM offers confidential support for families and friends of drug users, and helpful written information. Call their National Helpline on 020 7928 8900, email them at admin@adfam.org.uk or look at www.adfam.org.uk.

Alateen and **Al-Anon** are 24-hour services for young people who think they have a drinking problem or are worried about someone close to them. Their 24-hour helpline is 020 7403 0888.

Look in the Yellow Pages under "A" for your local branch of **Alcoholics Anonymous**.

Quit is the charity for people who want to stop smoking. You can call their helpline on 0800 002200, visit their website at www.quit.org.uk or email them for personal help on stopsmoking@quit.org.uk.

4

Your money

Managing your money

IN THIS SECTION:

The thing everyone knows about money is that you never have enough! But if you budget carefully and keep an eye on what you spend, you can make the best of what you've got.

Financial support

Your income (the money you have to live on) will come from one or more of the following:

● Social services

● Welfare benefits (e.g. income support, job seekers allowance)

● Training allowances

● Student grants

● Part-time wages

● Full-time wages

Your Personal Adviser, carer or social worker will be able to help you find out which benefits you may be entitled to.

Benefits can change, so for up-to-date information contact:

● **Your local Welfare Rights Officer**

● **Citizens Advice Bureau (CAB)**

● **The Department for Work and Pensions (England, Scotland and Wales)**

● **The Department for Social Development (Northern Ireland)**

Knowing how to manage your money – also called budgeting – is an important skill. It can save you a lot of worry and stop you from getting into debt.

Planning your budget

Think about:

● **What do you need to spend money on each week?**

● **Where will the money come from?**

- **Will it be enough?**

- **What can you do if you need more money?**

The things you may spend money on include:

- **Rent**

- **Bills, e.g. electricity, gas, TV licence**

- **Food**

- **Clothes and shoes**

- **Personal items, e.g. toothpaste, shampoo, deodorant**

- **Household items, e.g. toilet roll, cleaning products**

- **Travel, e.g. bus and train fares**

- **Phone, e.g. buying top-up cards or paying monthly contracts**

- **Things you need for study, e.g. text books, notepads and pens**

- **Things you need to help you apply for jobs, e.g. writing paper, envelopes and stamps, photocopying charges**

- **Going out to the cinema, clubs or for a meal**

- **Taxis for getting home late**

- **Hobbies, memberships and entrance fees, e.g. going swimming, kick-boxing classes**

- **Special occasions, e.g. having a party or planning a celebration meal**

- **Buying CDs and buying/renting DVDs**

- **Buying cards and presents (birthdays, Christmas, etc)**

- **Drinks**

How much money will you have to spend on these things? Will you have money for treats and special occasions each week, or will you need to save up for these? Most 16- and 17-year-olds receive under £50 a week, but you will probably get your housing paid for.

Getting some practice

A good way to think about how you'll manage in the future is to start budgeting now. And save some money if you can. At the moment you're probably getting an allowance from the council to cover the things you need and help you prepare for the future. To prevent you being tempted to spend it all, you could ask your foster carer or an older person you trust to help you open a bank account.

Think about the amount you need to spend each week and decide how much you need. Keep the rest and put it in your bank account.

Making your money go further

Are there ways you can save money? For example:

● When the weather is fine, walk or cycle instead of catching the bus.

● Get a season travel card if you use public transport regularly.

● Take-away food can be expensive so try to cook your own meals and prepare your own sandwiches. Can you buy in bulk with some other people? This is often cheaper.

● Late-night corner shops are often expensive – avoid regularly buying food or other products here.

● Only buy things you can pay for up front (from the money you have in your pocket). Try not to buy things on credit.

● Wear more clothes rather than turning up the heating, and put draught excluders around doors and windows.

● Don't buy the first thing you see – shop around. Buying second-hand may save you money.

● Buy clothes that will last, and which won't go out of fashion too quickly.

● Don't waste money on silly things you'll soon get bored with.

Opening a bank account

WE'VE GOT CURRENT ACCOUNTS, DEPOSIT ACCOUNTS AND SAVINGS ACCOUNTS BUT WE HAVEN'T GOT A 'TAKE AS MUCH AS YOU LIKE OUT WITHOUT PUTTING ANYTHING IN' ACCOUNT!

IN THIS SECTION:

1   Opening a bank account
2   Types of bank accounts

Opening a bank account

Even if you only have a small amount of money, keeping it in a bank or Post Office is a good idea. You'll be able to keep track of how much you have, and will still be able to get to it fairly easily. Your money may also earn interest while it is in an account. It's important to choose your account carefully.

You need to decide which sort of account will suit your needs. Look on websites to see which accounts will earn the most interest. If you find this difficult, get someone else to help you. You can also go into banks and ask them for information about their accounts – you will find leaflets about different types of accounts and saving schemes. Don't make any instant decisions. Take the leaflets away and read them. If you don't understand something, ask questions.

To open an account, you need to go in first and ask which documents they will need to see, e.g. your birth certificate and proof of your address. Make sure you have these with you when you go back to fill in the forms. If you have problems with the forms, ask the people working in the bank or Post Office for help.

Types of bank accounts

Current accounts

Current accounts usually give you instant access to your money. Some banks will allow you to have an account at 16 but some will only let you open an account at 18. You will normally be given a cheque book and cash point/debit card to withdraw your money.

If you use your cheque book or cash point card to spend more than the money you have put into your current account, you will have to pay a penalty charge. You may also get your account cancelled. You will only be allowed an "overdraft" (i.e. the bank allows you to spend more than you have but it is a fixed sum and you can't spend more than that) when you have proved that you are able to manage your money responsibly.

Deposit accounts

Deposit accounts are normally used for longer term savings, or for money you don't need instant access to. You have to apply five days in advance to get your money out of some deposit accounts.

Post Office accounts – National Savings Investment Account

These are like bank deposit accounts, so check how easy it will be to get your money out.

Post Office Accounts – National Giro Bank Account

This works like a current account and you can have access to your money instantly.

HELPFUL HINT

A debit card allows you to spend money you have already paid into your account, so you can use this as part of your budget.

A credit card allows you to spend money you don't have, so you get charged interest on this. But it can seem like free money – so you may be tempted to spend. Don't – you could run up big debts and you will have to pay interest on this, i.e. you will have to pay more money because you haven't cleared your debts and paid what you owe.

Credit cards, agreements and contracts

IN THIS SECTION:

1 **Credit cards and store cards**
2 **Signing up to contracts**
3 **Useful organisations**

Credit cards and store cards

These allow you to spend money you don't have. You then have to make a payment each month to pay back this money you have spent. You will be charged high rates of interest for this service if you don't pay back on time or if you only pay some of the money you owe (the "outstanding balance"). Credit cards and store cards are an easy way of getting into serious debt. Banks and stores are usually keen to encourage you to get credit because it means they sell more products and can charge you interest. They may seem like they are doing you a favour – but it's really the other way around!

You cannot have a credit card until you are 18, but it's best to avoid getting one at all unless you really need it and feel confident that you can manage it. Credit cards are one of the reasons so many people run up huge debts.

Signing up to contracts

When you have worked out how much money you have to live on and what you need to budget for, you need to work out the most "cost effective" (cheapest) ways of buying what you need or want. This sometimes involves signing up to contracts.

It's tempting to sign up for lots of services and products. But remember, it all adds up and eats into the amount of money you will have to spend each month.

Before you sign up for any services, such as a phone contract, a repair service or a hire service, you need to do the following.

● **Listen to/read carefully the words of the agreements that you will be signing up to. Make sure you are happy with this and can meet the conditions set out.**

● **If there is anything you're not sure about ask questions before you sign. Don't sign anything you are not sure about. Ask someone you trust to help you if there are lots of words you don't understand.**

● **Think about what you are going to get for your money. Is this a good deal, or could you get a better one somewhere else?**

● **How long does the contract last for?**

- What are the terms for getting out of the agreement?

- Will you have to pay a penalty if you want to stop the contract?

- Are you sure you can afford to make the payments every month (or four or six months)?

- Do you really need it, or do you just fancy it?

 NAS'S STORY

When you realise you can get stuff on credit it's like – wey-hey, man! I was working and I got this credit card and cards for a couple of big stores and things. We also got this DVD player for the house and this wide-screen TV. Then I started getting hassle at work and one day I couldn't take it any more. I just walked out. It was months before I got another job, but there was all these bills to pay. They kept coming in each month. It was scary. In the end I got some advice from the Citizens Advice Bureau. They helped me sort stuff out. Now I think twice before I sign up for anything.

Useful organisations

For England, Scotland and Wales you can visit the **Department for Work and Pensions** website at www.dwp.gov.uk for details on benefits.

In Northern Ireland **The Social Security Agency** is part of the Department for Social Development. The website address is www.dsdni.gov.uk

The **Citizens Advice Bureau** website has advice on a whole range of benefits and how to find your nearest office. Visit them on www.citizensadvice.org.uk.

www.need2know.co.uk is a website for young people that gives advice about all sorts of things – including money.

5

Your education and training

School or college?

IN THIS SECTION:

When you reach 16 you have several choices to make about your future:

1 **To stay on at school**

2 **Leave school and find a job**

3 **Go on a training course**

4 **Do something different – like travel or become a volunteer**

You need to start thinking about these choices.

Connexions and careers advisers

At the start of this book we told you about Connexions. This is a service that provides all 13–19-year-olds in England with information and guidance about the choices open to them. Your school should arrange meetings for you with your Connexions Adviser, but you can also contact the Connexions service directly yourself.

If you live in Scotland, Wales or Northern Ireland, there are different career services which you can use. Ask your school, your social worker, Personal Adviser or foster carer about these.

Staying on at school

Maybe you haven't enjoyed school that much and you want to leave as soon as possible, but there can be good reasons for staying on. It's worth thinking about these.

● **Getting qualifications can be a big help in finding a job.**

● **You may need certain qualifications for the particular job or training course you want to do.**

● **Education can open up opportunities you might otherwise miss out on.**

● **Do you want to go to university? If so, you will need some qualifications to get in.**

Sixth form or local college?

The good things about most sixth forms and local colleges are:

- **You don't have to have passed exams to get in.**

- **They offer practical courses that lead to employment.**

- **Some courses have work-based placements so you can get used to the job while you are studying.**

Full- or part-time study?

Sometimes studying part time can be the best option. You might find it easier to manage a part-time course. Studying part-time also means that you can claim some social security benefits while you study. It also means that it may take longer before you are able to start work and earn your living. You need to weigh up the options carefully with help from your Connexions Adviser, your Personal Adviser or your social worker.

If you choose part-time study you can only study for 16 hours (or less) at school/college a week or it will affect your social security benefits. The rules differ slightly for students who are single parents or have a disability.

You may also be able to claim some other allowances to pay for your education. Talk to your Connexions Adviser or careers adviser about this.

HELPFUL HINT

Don't set yourself up to fail by choosing a course that expects you to do lots of things you find difficult. Also, think about how long the course lasts and the different parts of it. You might enjoy Year 1 but if it's a three year course, will you still enjoy Years 2 and 3 and be able to keep up with the amount of studying involved? Choose something that allows you to use your skills well and matches the way you work best, to give yourself the best chance of succeeding.

Disabled students

There are laws in England, Scotland and Wales (The Disability Discrimination Act 1995) that say that it is against the law for you to be treated less favourably than another student because of your disability. New laws were being introduced in Northern Ireland at the time this guide was published.

Colleges and schools must show that they have made "reasonable adjustments" so that you are not disadvantaged. This includes things like providing someone to help you with particular physical problems or making some changes to the surroundings. However, the law only expects them to make reasonable changes, so you may find that some schools and colleges will say that they are not able to meet your needs properly, so will not offer you a place.

If you think that the school or college is not prepared to make enough effort to meet your needs (within the requirements of the law) and is treating you less favourably because of your disability, you can challenge this. You should seek help from your Connexions Adviser, or from an organisation like the Citizens Advice Bureau or the Disability Rights Commission.

HELPFUL HINT

The Disability Rights Commission (DRC) was set up to promote equality and prevent discrimination against disabled people in England, Scotland and Wales. Their website www.drc-gb.org has useful information about disabled students and the law.

You can also contact the DRC Helpline on 0845 622 633 for information and advice about how to make a claim against a school, college (or other organisation) which you feel has discriminated against you.

In Northern Ireland you can contact the Equality Commission for Northern Ireland on 02890 500 600 or by Textphone on 02890 500 589, or by email at information@equalityni.org. Their website is www.equalityni.org.

Courses you can do

IN THIS SECTION:

Work-based training for young people (WBTYP)

WBTYP is a government training scheme for 16–17-year-olds living in England and Wales.

If you are not working you can stay on a WBTYP scheme until you are 18 years old.

You will get a basic weekly allowance, but you cannot work for more than 40 hours a week. You may be able to get other social security benefits on top of the weekly basic allowance.

A great advantage of the scheme is that you will get more support than if you went straight into the job. Most courses offer extra help with reading, writing and maths.

Your Connexions Adviser will help you register for a WBTYP placement if this is what you choose, or if you lose your job and can't get another one.

Modern Apprenticeships

Modern Apprenticeships are three-year, work-based training programmes for 16–17-year-olds to learn skills and gain qualifications. They are for young people living in England, Scotland and Wales.

Open University

The Open University offers short courses (minimum age 16) to degree courses (minimum age 18) which you study at home, in your own time.

Costs

Local Education Authorities (LEAs) sometimes give grants for living costs, course materials and travel. If you are in care or have been in care, you can ask your local authority to fund you.

There are also some funding schemes available. Below are two examples of these – but be aware that names for benefits do change, and that different nations in the UK have different ways of funding students.

Learner support fund

Learner support funds are available for students in the UK who face financial problems which might stop them taking part in education. These can be costs for things like travel, books, equipment, childcare and accommodation.

People who are most likely to get learner support fund are young people leaving care, people with disabilities and/or learning difficulties, or students who reach the age of 19 and lose their benefits while they are still studying.

Education maintenance allowance

If you are doing A levels or a "vocational course" (a course that is likely to lead to a career) and live in England, you are probably entitled to Education Maintenance Allowance (EMA). You receive around £10–30 a week depending on your circumstances. This money is paid directly into your bank account and is meant to cover things like books, equipment and travel for your course. You can also earn "bonuses" (up to about £500) if you can show you are making good progress on your course and are very committed to your studies.

Your Personal Adviser, Connexions Adviser or careers adviser will be able to find out what financial support you are entitled to. There are also websites where you can look up some of this information for yourself (see Useful Organisations).

Finding the right course for you

Your Connexions Adviser, Personal Adviser or careers adviser should be able to give you all the information you need about courses and training placements available. They will help you think about what will be right for you. You can also do some investigating yourself by looking on the websites of colleges and reading about the courses.

When you are choosing a course, you need to think about:

● **What are you good at?**

● **What subjects do you enjoy?**

- What job would you like to do when you finish and will this course help you achieve this?

- Can you easily get to where the course is held?

- Will the course involve a lot of extra things that will cost money, such as having to provide your own tools/equipment, special clothing, books?

- Is the course mainly practical based (demonstrating skills as you go along) or are there a lot of reading and written assignments?

Applying for a college or training placement

When you have decided which course or training placement you would like to apply for, you need to:

- Contact the college you have chosen and ask for a copy of the course and "college prospectus" (information booklet about the college) as this will give you a lot of important information including how and when you need to apply for the course.

- If you have any questions, or there are things you are unsure of, phone the college and ask to speak to someone from "admissions" or a tutor or trainer from the course or department.

- Find out how to apply for the course you want to do. Usually you need to fill in a form or write a letter, but you may be asked to go for an interview.

- Make sure you fill in any forms, or write any letters, very carefully. Write what you want to say in rough first and when you are happy with this, copy or type it onto the form or letter. They are more likely to choose someone who has put time and effort into preparing their form or letter.

- Most colleges have a closing date for applications. Make sure you find out when this is and make sure your application gets there before that date.

Visiting a college/training centre

Most colleges have open days when you can go and look around and chat to the course leaders and people currently doing the course. You can also make an appointment to visit the college at another time if there is not an open day coming up.

- **Think about the questions you are going to ask, e.g. what sort of accommodation is there? What leisure facilities do they have? What support is available?**

- **Be prepared to answer questions about why you want to do the course you are applying for. Plan a good answer that shows your enthusiasm and commitment.**

- **Present yourself well. Make sure your clothes are clean and appropriate (better to go a bit smarter if you're not sure what to wear) and think about how you behave and what you say. You want to create a good impression.**

 LEON'S STORY

Since I was a kid I wanted to work in a big hotel. Be a cook or something. Someone told me you had to do a chef's course. Lisa – she's my pathway plan worker – kept asking 'why do you want to do this?' It really narked me. She sent off for this stuff from the college and we looked at one session. It was a big revelation. I'd never realised you had to study so much. Lisa said maybe I should do a catering course instead. Something a bit shorter. But what I'm really good at is computers so we're going to look at some of those courses as well.

Volunteering or taking "time out"

Perhaps you don't want to settle down to a job or college course straight away and would be interested in spending a year or two doing something different. That way you can learn more about yourself and what you might want to do, and also some employers welcome someone who has broadened their experience in life. If you are seriously thinking about "time out" at any stage, why not consider the following?

- **Community Service Volunteers (CSV): If you are over 16, you could become a full time volunteer working on a range of interesting projects for between 4–12 months. Volunteers** receive board, pocket money and paid holidays as well as support from the organisation.

● **Prince's Trust Volunteers:** If you are 16–25 you could gain useful experience and skills through teamwork in the community.

● **Voluntary Service Overseas (VSO):** If you are 18 or over and would like to work on a project helping people in another country, applying to VSO is an option.

Useful organisations

www.need2know.co.uk is a website for young people that gives advice about all sorts of things – including education and training.

www.Connexions.gov.uk is a website for 13–19-year-olds which offers you information and advice about education and careers.

You can also contact Connexions advisers by phone on 0808 001 3219, by text on 0776 641 3219, by Textphone on 0800 096 8336 or by email through the website.

www.Support4learning.org.uk contains lots of useful information about student life. It has lots of information about funding.

Your work

IN THIS SECTION:

Getting a good job at 16 or 17 isn't easy. You need to think carefully whether it's best to stay in some form of education or training to help you prepare better for the world of work. But there are some young people who do make a success of going straight from school to work because they are prepared to work hard and make it succeed for them. You have to go for one or the other – work or further education/training – so get all the help and advice you need to make the right choice for you.

To help you decide whether you are ready to get a job, you need to bear these things in mind.

● **Most employers expect you to have had some form of training or qualification.**

● **Most employers are looking for someone with experience (which is why doing a course which offers workplace training can be helpful).**

● **Without qualifications and experience you probably won't earn very much.**

● **Very few people start off in their "dream job". Many people start off in any job they can get and then work their way up.**

● **If you do go straight into work you need to work hard and stick with the job, until you have enough experience to go up the next rung of the ladder.**

 NEAL'S STORY

My mate's dad has a garage and I've wanted to work with cars since I was little. My mate always said there was a job for me in the garage when I left school. But when I got there I found that they wanted me to work for, like, no money at all. I got all the dirty boring jobs like sweeping up. Nobody took the time to show me anything so I wasn't learning much. Then my sister's bloke, who's a mechanic, said I should think about getting some proper training. I applied for college and I did a proper course. My mate's dad said he'd employ me again when I finished. And it was better like that. I got better money and more respect. Now me and my brother-in-law are setting up a business together. It's good that I got that experience.

Looking for a job

Where to look:

- The local job centre

- Local papers

- Ask friends

- Look for adverts in windows of shops and restaurants

- Go along to companies and ask if there are any vacancies

- Register with an employment agency – you can find contact numbers in the Yellow Pages

How to apply:

- If you apply through a job centre, the centre will contact the employer on your behalf and make an appointment for you to go for an interview.

- If you respond to an advert, it will tell you how to apply, e.g. ring for an application form, send your CV or write a letter.

- If you ask in a shop, factory, restaurant, etc, about vacancies they may put your name on a list and contact you if a job becomes available. You may still have to apply in writing or go to an interview.

- If you register with an employment agency, they will contact you if they have work available, or you can phone them regularly to ask this.

What will an employer want to know?

- What qualifications you have

- What experience you have

- What you can bring to the job that's different from someone else

- Whether you will be someone who will be good to employ, e.g. will you be on time, polite, use your initiative, work well with other people?

Filling in an application form

If you have to fill in an application form or write a letter, you need to do the following:

● Read the "person specification" (the bit about what kind of person the employer is looking for) and any other information you are given about the job. Are you the kind of person they are looking for?

● It's good to be ambitious, but it's silly to waste time applying for a job which requires far more experience than you have.

● Make sure you read the whole of the application form before you start filling it in.

● Follow very carefully any information they give you about how to apply for the job. If it says fill in a form, then do this! Don't send a CV instead. Your application may not be considered if you do.

● Fill in the form using your neatest writing. Usually you need to use a black ink pen.

● If you are filling in a form online make sure you spell-check it carefully.

● If the online form isn't working, ring or email the organisation and tell them you are having a problem with it. Don't miss out on your chance to apply for the job.

● Make sure you include any extra information they ask for, e.g. a certificate to show you have attended a training course, a copy of your driving licence, your birth certificate. Don't send the original document unless this is essential – take a photocopy. If you have to send an original document, either take it there yourself or put the letter in registered post – this is a special service you pay for at the Post Office, to make sure that your letter is delivered safely.

● Make sure you send or hand in your application form by the date required. If you don't, your application probably won't be considered.

HELPFUL HINTS

- Never lie on an application form. You're bound to get found out and you can be sacked on the spot. You may not be entitled to any benefits if this happens.

- Think about how to put the skills and experience you have across in the best ways possible. For example, 'I am a member of the committee at my local youth club. This has taught me how to take part in meetings, how to plan events and how to work as part of a team'.

Creating a good CV

Some employers ask to see your CV – which is short for "curriculum vitae". This means a summary of the details of your life, but what they are really looking for is details of your education, achievements and work experience.

There's lots of advice on the internet about how to create a good CV and your Connexions Adviser or careers adviser will also give you help with this.

A good CV includes:

- Your name, address, contact telephone number and an email address if you have one.

- A personal profile – this gives a short description of who you are and the qualities you could bring to the job, e.g. 'I am a hardworking and dedicated person who really loves being with children. I have studied child development and I want to work in a nursery so I can help young children develop to the best of their ability.'

- Your skills and achievements, e.g. a mentor for children in years 1 and 2. Received an excellent report for my work placement at Springfield Nursery.

- Education – give the name of your school and the dates you have been there, e.g. 1999–2005. Then list any subjects you have taken and the grades you received. Also show any subjects you are currently studying for.

- Work experience – list any part-time jobs, holiday jobs or work placements. Give a brief description of the role, e.g. 'Swimming pool attendant (Saturdays and school holidays). Working with the public to keep the pool safe. Working closely with other members of the leisure centre team.'

- Any other relevant experience, e.g. if you are a volunteer or member of a local committee. Give a brief description of this and say what you did, e.g. 'Member of the carnival committee – helped to plan the event and worked with local children to design and make costumes.'

- Activities and interests – give details of your hobbies and interests, e.g. I enjoy boxercise, karate and pilates and go to classes each week. I like painting and crafts.

- Referees – give the names and contact details of people like tutors and employers who can say what you can do.

Top tips for creating a good CV

- Organise the information carefully into sections.

- Don't make it too long or include lots of unnecessary info like height, your health history or whether you are married or not.

- Check there are no spelling errors.

- Set the information out clearly, in a way that looks professional.

- Don't go for anything too fancy like photos and elaborate typefaces – it's not necessary. What matters is the information you give about yourself.

- Get someone else to check your CV – they may spot something you've missed.

Going to interviews

Most employers want to meet people at interviews before they offer a job. Often they will interview several people for the same job, so you need to make sure you give yourself the best chance to be picked over everyone else.

So what do I need to do?

● Dress smartly.

● Be clean and smell fresh.

● Talk clearly. Be polite.

● Smile – it will make you feel less nervous.

● Listen carefully and answer questions sensibly.

● Think about the way you sit. Don't slouch or lie in the chair but don't perch nervously on the edge. Just sit upright with your shoulders relaxed.

● Try not to fidget. Put your hands in your lap or on the arms of the chair and keep them still.

● If you get tongue-tied or say the wrong thing, it's not the end of the world. Just say 'Sorry, that didn't come out right. Let me say that again.'

DON'T WORRY ABOUT BEING NERVOUS. MOST PEOPLE FIND INTERVIEWS A BIT SCARY!

Be well prepared

Before you go to an interview you need to make sure you are fully prepared.

● Find out as much as you can about the job and the organisation.

● Think about the sort of questions they might ask you and what sort of answers you will give.

● Often you will be asked if you have any questions of your own. Prepare some questions which show you have thought about the job, e.g. 'It says in the job description that there will be opportunities to work with the public. What sort of opportunities will these be?'

● Allow yourself plenty of time to get to the interview.

● If you feel very nervous before the interview, concentrate on breathing very slowly.

HELPFUL HINT

If the nerves are very bad before the interview, ask where the toilet is. Go there and put your arms down by your sides. Slowly bring your arms up in front of you. When they are about shoulder height open them out slowly – until you are standing in the shape of the letter T. Then slowly bring them down by your side. Concentrate on breathing slowly as you do this. This exercise opens up your lungs and lets lots of oxygen into them. It can help you to feel a lot calmer.

Keeping your job

Once you have a job it is important to make sure you are a good employee, as you will stand more chance of being promoted or moving on to better jobs, being given more responsibilities, developing new skills and earning more money. Some things you can do are:

- Always be on time.
- Make sure you do everything you are supposed to do that day.
- Be polite and helpful.
- Let people know what you are achieving.
- Discuss any problems with your employer/line manager or someone from Human Resources, e.g. if you are being bullied.
- Take any opportunities you can to develop your skills.

HELPFUL HINT

Once you have a job it's important to try and stick with it. Employers will want to know why you didn't stay in your previous job. It's best only to leave a job when you have found something better to move on to.

Jobs are not easy to find and the longer you stay in a job the more financial security you will have and the better it will look on your CV. Most people don't get their perfect job when they first start working – you have to work your way up by getting the right experience.

National Insurance numbers

Everyone needs a National Insurance number in order to work or claim benefits. Young people who are living at home when they are 16 usually have this sent to them automatically. If you are living away from home, your social worker will often arrange for you to be sent this. If you don't receive it, you need to apply to the Department for Work and Pensions. Get your foster carer, Connexions Adviser, careers adviser or someone like a mentor to help you with this.

Useful organisations

www.careers-Scotland has a helpful section on how to write a CV. There are also samples of CVs and tips on how to avoid common mistakes.

www.careers-gateway.co.uk has advice about filling in applications, writing CVs and going to interviews.

www.dwp.gov.uk is the website for the Department for Work and Pensions. They give lots of information about work and benefits. They are also the organisation to contact if you don't have a National Insurance number.

Planning ahead

IN THIS SECTION:

Being in control of your own life is one of the best ways to feel good about yourself. If your life is in a muddle you're much more likely to feel stressed. Sometimes just a simple thing like sorting out your room can make you feel loads better. It's also important to take control of your own behaviour so that relationships with friends, flatmates and work colleagues don't get "messy".

This section helps you look at some of the ways to organise your life, get along with other people and get any extra help or advice you need.

Staying in control

These are some basic hints to help you feel in control of your life.

● Don't let things get in a muddle. It's easier to sort things out as you go along.

● Try and keep paperwork sorted. Get some cheap cardboard or plastic files and label them so you can find things when you need them, e.g. bills to pay, bank account details, receipts and guarantees.

● Plan your time. Don't leave everything to the last minute.

● Be realistic. Don't set yourself impossible deadlines – you'll only panic and feel a failure if you do.

● Make notes and lists of important things you need to remember.

● Don't put off things that are worrying you. Get help and advice to sort them out.

● Get information. The more information you have about something, the more in control you feel.

● Feel in control of your money.

HELPFUL HINT

It's hard to organise your life if you don't have a diary, personal organiser or filofax. If you can't afford one, use a notebook and copy the dates down from a calendar or someone else's diary (ask permission first!). Leave a space under each date for appointments.

When you need some help

Do you have a problem? Or something you want to do and you need to know more about it? Maybe you just need a bit of extra information or advice to help you make an important decision.

- Think about who will be the best person or organisation to give you the help or information that you need, e.g. your Personal Adviser, Connexions Adviser, the council, your benefits adviser.

- When you have identified who may be able to help you, think about exactly what you want to know. What questions do you need to ask? It's often worth writing these down.

- Contact the person or organisation. They may be able to answer your questions on the phone. Or perhaps you need to make an appointment with them to discuss what you want to know.

HELPFUL HINT

Do your homework. If you're not sure which service will be the right one to help you, check out some websites. Find out what services different people offer. If a service doesn't offer exactly what you are looking for, it's often worth looking up the "links" part of their website where they list other useful organisations.

Making appointments over the phone

1 Before you phone, make sure you know when you will be free and when you can get there. Check you have the correct name of the person you need to see.

2 Say who is calling and ask politely if it is possible to make an appointment with that person.

3 If you have a problem with the time you are given for an appointment, explain politely that you cannot make this time, and ask for another time. If you are not sure that you can make the appointment time, write it down and explain that you need to check this and you will ring back when you have checked.

4   If you want someone to go with you to the appointment, say that you will be bringing someone with you.

5   At the end of the call, don't forget to say "thank you".

HELPFUL HINT

Sometimes getting through to the right person or department on the phone can be very frustrating. Allow yourself enough time because you may be held in a queue or have to wait while you get passed from person to person. Stay calm and polite – getting frazzled won't help. If you know you're going to be waiting on the phone for a long time, why not have a mug of tea and a magazine beside you?

Getting the best out of an appointment

● Write down the questions you want answers for.

● Don't be late. Allow enough time to get there.

● Be polite and friendly. If you treat people with respect they will treat you with respect.

● If you have made notes beforehand, get these out and put them somewhere you can see them.

● Make sure you explain clearly to the person you are meeting what you want to know. It's often helpful to explain why you need to know this, e.g. 'I'm not very happy with my course and I want to know what other courses I could change to.'

● Write notes during the meeting of things you need to remember, or ask the person you are meeting to write these down for you.

● If you haven't understood something, ask the person to explain it again.

● At the end of the appointment make sure you are clear about what happens next. (Maybe the meeting has answered all your questions, but maybe you or the person you are meeting needs to do something else.)

- If other things need to happen, do you know when this will be? Don't be afraid to ask.

- Say "'goodbye" and "thank you" to the person you have met with.

How to complain

If you are not happy with a service you have received, you are entitled to make a complaint. Make sure you think carefully about what it is you are complaining about. Not agreeing with the information someone has given you is not necessarily a reason to make an official complaint, unless this has caused you considerable difficulty as a result, for example, you lost out on something you were entitled to or you were injured or distressed as a direct result.

If you are complaining about a public service like the council, the NHS or Connexions, then you need to find out about their complaints procedures. Look on their website or phone them for information about this.

- Make sure you find out exactly what you need to do to complain, e.g. write a letter, fill in a form, speak to someone.

- Find out who you need to send this to, or get the name of the person you need to speak to.

- Make sure you explain exactly why you are complaining and include any evidence you have, such as dates of meetings and letters. (If you send any documents, photocopy these first and keep the original copy yourself.)

- Get someone you trust to check what you are planning to send or say. They may be able to suggest a better way of explaining what you mean.

- You will probably get a letter to say that your complaint has been received. But it often takes a while for complaints to be investigated, so be patient.

- You should always be told the outcome of your complaint and what decision has been reached.

- If you are still not happy with this response, find out how you can take this further. Again, be sure to follow the correct procedures.

● **If you don't follow the right complaints procedure your complaint probably won't be heard or taken seriously.**

Advocates

If you need help making a complaint about a service, or just feel that people aren't listening to you properly, you may be able to get the help of an advocate. This is someone who puts your point of view across to other people on your behalf. All councils should have advocacy services for young people who are, or have recently, been in care. Ask your Personal Adviser or social worker about this service.

Useful organisations

The National Youth Advocacy Service (England and Wales) offers advice, information, support and representation to children and young people when they want their wishes and feelings taken into account. The organisation can be contacted at www.nyas.net or on their confidential legal advice line 0800 616101.

8

Useful addresses

Useful names, addresses and organisations

General help and advice

Albert Kennedy Trust
Runs schemes to find foster carers, lodgings and housing for lesbian, gay and bisexual young people.
Unit 305a Hatton Square
16/16a Baldwin Gardens
London EC1N 7RJ
Tel: 020 7831 6562
www.akt.org.uk

Care for Life
A Christian charity which provides a number of social caring and educational projects for young people.
53 Romney Street
London SW1P 3RF
Tel: 020 7233 0455
www.care.org.uk

Childline
A free and confidential 24-hour helpline for children and young people.
45 Folgate Street
London E1 6GL
Freephone: 0800 1111
www.childline.org.uk

Children's Legal Centre
Provides legal advice and information to children, young people and their carers.
University of Essex
Wivenhoe Park
Colchester CO4 3SQ
Freephone: 0800 783 2187
www.childrenslegalcentre.com

Citizens Advice Bureaux
Provides free, independent information and advice on legal, money and other problems.
Myddleton House
115–123 Pentonville Road
London N1 9LZ
Tel: 020 7833 2181
www.citizensadvice.org.uk

Connexions
Offers advice on education, careers, housing, money and health for 13–19-year-olds.
Freephone: 0808 001 3219
www.connexions.gov.uk

Crimestoppers
Works to help identify, prevent, solve and reduce crime. Anyone can contact them anonymously to report details of crime.
Freephone: 0800 555 111
www.crimestoppers-uk.org

Cruse
Provides bereavement care for anyone who has been affected by a death.
Cruse House
126 Sheen Road
Richmond TW1 1UR
Freephone: 0808 808 1677
www.crusebereavementcare.org.uk

Eating Disorders Association
Provides information and advice
on all aspects of eating disorders.
103 Prince of Wales Road
Norwich NR1 1DW
Tel: 0845 634 7650
4.30pm–8.30pm Mon–Fri
Youthline for under 19s
www.edauk.com

Lesbian and Gay Switchboard
A 24-hour helpline offering
support, advice and information to
lesbians, gay men and bisexuals.
Tel: 020 7837 7324
www.llgs.org.uk

MIND
Works to advance the views and
needs of people with mental
health problems, and provides
advice and support.
15–19 Broadway
London E15 4BQ
Tel: 0845 766 0163
9.15am–5.15pm Mon–Fri
www.mind.org.uk

**NACRO (National Association for
the Care and Resettlement of
Offenders)**
Helps ex-offenders and their
families to improve their lives
and futures.
169 Clapham Road
London SW9 0PU
Tel: 020 7582 6500
www.nacro.org.uk

National Debt Line
Provides free, confidential and
independent advice on dealing
with debt problems.
Tricorn House

51–53 Hagley Road
Edgbaston
Birmingham B16 8TP
Freephone: 0808 080 4000
www.nationaldebtline.co.uk

Rape Crisis Centre
Look in Yellow Pages under 'R'
for your local branch.

Refuge
Provides a 24-hour domestic
violence helpline for women and
children, and a network of safe
houses.
Freephone: 0808 200 0247
www.refuge.org.uk

Refugee Council
Offers help and support to
asylum seekers and refugees.
240–250 Ferndale Road
London SW9 8BB
Tel: 020 7346 6700
www.refugeecouncil.org.uk

Shelter
Provides a 24-hour national
housing service.
88 Old Street
London EC1V 9HU
Freephone: 0808 800 4444
www.shelter.org.uk

Women's Aid
Works to end domestic violence
against women and children, and
provides help and advice.
Head Office
PO Box 391
Bristol BS99 7WS
Freephone: 0808 200 0247
www.womensaid.org.uk

Care leavers

CareLaw.org.uk
A website which provides information on rights and legal matters for young people in care or leaving care.
www.carelaw.org.uk

Care Leaver's Association
Offers support, information, help with accessing childhood case records, and aims to raise public awareness of care leavers' needs.
The Care Leavers Association
St Thomas Centre
Ardwick Green North
Manchester M12 6FZ
Tel: 0161 275 9500
www.careleavers.com

Care Leavers Reunited
A website run by the Care Leaver's Association to help those who have been in care to make contact with past friends.
www.careleaversreunited.com

LeavingHome.info
An online guide to leaving care and housing for young people in Scotland, run by the Scottish Council for Single Homeless.
www.leavinghome.info

A National Voice
Campaigns for the rights of care leavers, and offers advice and information.
A National Voice
Central Hall
Oldham Street
Manchester M1 1JQ
Tel: 0161 237 5577
www.anationalvoice.org

Sexual health and pregnancy

Brook Advisory Centre
Provides confidential sexual health advice and free contraception to young people up to the age of 25.
421 Highgate Studios
53–79 Highgate Road
London NW5 1TL
Freephone:0800 018 5023
Helpline: 0800 292 930
              advice for under 19s

**FPA
(Family Planning Association)**
Offers help, advice and information on contraception and sexual health.
50 Featherstone Street
London EC1Y 8QU
Tel: 0845 310 1334
9am–6pm Mon–Fri
www.fpa.org.uk

National AIDS Helpline
A 24-hour helpline for anyone affected by AIDS.
Freephone: 0800 567 123

Terrence Higgins Trust
Provides advice and information
on HIV and AIDS.
314–320 Gray's Inn Road
London WC1X 8DP
Tel: 0845 122 1200
10am–10pm Mon–Fri
12noon–6pm Sat–Sun
www.tht.org.uk/

Drugs and alcohol

Adfam
Offers confidential support for
families and friends of drug
users.
Tel: 020 7553 7640
www.adfam.org.uk

**Alateen and Al-Anon Family
Groups**
Services for young people and
families who think they may have
a drinking problem or are
worried about someone close to
them.
Tel: 020 7403 0888
10am–10pm
www.al-anonuk.org.uk

Alcoholics Anonymous
A service for anyone who thinks
they may have a drinking
problem.
Tel: 0845 769 7555
www.alcoholics-
anonymous.org.uk

Drugscope
Provides information on drugs.
32–36 Loman Street
London SE1 0EE
Tel: 020 7928 1211
www.drugscope.org.uk

National Drugs Helpline
Provides information and advice
on drugs.
Freephone: 0800 776 600
www.talktofrank.com

Quit
Provides advice, help and
information for all those trying to
give up smoking.
Ground Floor
211 Old Street
London EC1V 9NR
Freephone: 0800 002 200
www.quit.org.uk

Education, employment and volunteering

Community Service Volunteers
Provides information and organises volunteer projects across the UK.
237 Pentonville Road
London N1 9NJ
Tel: 020 7278 6601
www.csv.org.uk

Open University
PO Box 197
Milton Keynes MK7 6BJ
Tel: 0870 333 4340
www.open.ac.uk

Princes Trust Volunteers
Provides advice and practical support for young people aged 14–30 to realise their potential.
18 Park Square East
London NW1 4LH
Tel: 020 7543 1234
www.princes-trust.org.uk

SKILL
Promotes opportunities for young people with any disability in post-16 education, training and work.
Chapter House
18–20 Crucifix Lane
London SE1 3JW
Freephone: 0800 328 5050
www.skill.org.uk

Voluntary Service Overseas
Organises voluntary work placements overseas.
317 Putney Bridge Road
London SW15 2PN
Tel: 020 8780 7200
www.vso.org.uk

General help and projects for people being fostered or adopted

Barnardo's
Offers a wide range of support services for children, young people and families.
Tanners Lane
Barkingside
Ilford IG6 1QG
Tel: 020 8550 8822
www.barnardos.org.uk

The Children's Society
Provides help and advice for children and young people.
Edward Rudolf House
Margery Street
London WC1X 0JL
Tel: 020 7841 4400
www.the-childrens-society.org.uk

The Fostering Network Young People's Project (England and Wales)
Works with young people on a number of projects aimed at allowing young people's voices to be heard.
87 Blackfriars Road
London SE1 8HA
Tel: 020 7620 6412
www.fostering.net/england/youngpeople.php

The Fostering Network Young People's Project (Scotland)
Second Floor
Ingram House
227 Ingram Street
Glasgow G1 1DA
Tel: 0141 204 1400
www.fostering.net/scotland/young_people/

National Children's Bureau – Young NCB
A free membership network for children and young people aged 17 and under which gives members the chance to speak out on important issues.
8 Wakely Street
London EC1V 7QE
Tel: 020 7843 6000
www.ncb.org.uk
Young NCB:
www.ncb.org.uk/page.asp?sve=786

The Scottish Throughcare and Aftercare Forum
Aims to improve support for young people leaving care in Scotland by consulting with young people and workers.
Second Floor
37 Otago Street
Glasgow G12 8JJ
Tel: 0141 357 4124
www.scottishthroughcare.org.uk/youth/index.asp

Voice (formerly Voice for the Child in Care)
Works with children and young people in care to support them and promote their views.
Unit 4, Pride Court
80–82 White Lion Street
London N1 9PF
Freephone: 0808 800 5792
www.vcc-uk.org

The Who Cares? Trust
Aims to improve the lives of children and young people in residential and foster care. Runs CareZone, an interactive online network for young people in care.
Kemp House
152–160 City Road
London EC1V 2NP
Tel: 020 7251 3117
www.thewhocarestrust.org.uk
CareZone:
www.thewhocarestrust.org.uk/carezone.htm

My Personal Information

First name(s): ....

Surname: ....

Preferred name if different from above: ....

Date of birth: ....

My National Insurance Number: ....

My address is: ....

....

....

My telephone number is: ....

My mobile number is: ....

My email address is: ....

My birth certificate is kept: ....

My passport number is: ....

My medical registration NHS number is: ....

My doctor's name is: ....

My doctor's address is: ....

....

....

My doctor's telephone number is: ....

My dentist's name is: ....

My optician's name is: ....

My landlord's name is: ....

My school/college address is: ....

....

....

My school/college telephone number is: ....

My tutor's name is: ....

My work address is: ....

....

....

My boss's name is: ....

My social worker's name is: ....

My social worker can be contacted at: ....

My emergency contact is: ....

Useful addresses & telephone numbers

Name	**Name** ....
Address	Address ....
....	....
....	....
Post code	Post code ....
Telephone	Telephone ....
Mobile	Mobile ....
Email	Email ....
Name	**Name** ....
Address	Address ....
....	....
....	....
Post code	Post code ....
Telephone	Telephone ....
Mobile	Mobile ....
Email	Email ....
Name	**Name** ....
Address	Address ....
....	....
....	....
Post code	Post code ....
Telephone	Telephone ....
Mobile	Mobile ....
Email	Email ....
Name	**Name** ....
Address	Address ....
....	....
....	....
Post code	Post code ....
Telephone	Telephone ....
Mobile	Mobile ....
Email	Email ....

Name ....
Address ....
....
....
Post code ....
Telephone............................
Mobile ....
Email...................................

Name.................................
Address ....
....
....
Post code.............................
Telephone.............................
Mobile..................................
Email ....

Name ....
Address ....
....
....
Post code ....
Telephone............................
Mobile ....
Email...................................

Name.................................
Address ....
....
....
Post code.............................
Telephone.............................
Mobile..................................
Email ....

Name ....
Address ....
....
....
Post code ....
Telephone............................
Mobile ....
Email...................................

Name.................................
Address ....
....
....
Post code.............................
Telephone.............................
Mobile..................................
Email ....

Name ....
Address ....
....
....
Post code ....
Telephone............................
Mobile ....
Email...................................

Name.................................
Address ....
....
....
Post code.............................
Telephone.............................
Mobile..................................
Email ....